50
to Stand Up
for™ America

*Put the Spirit of July 4th
into Everyday Life*

W. B. FREEMAN

STARBURST PUBLISHERS®

P. O. Box 4123, Lancaster, Pennsylvania 17604

To schedule author appearances, write:
Author Appearances
Starburst Promotions
P.O. Box 4123
Lancaster, PA 17604
or call 717-293-0939.

CREDITS:
Cover design by David Marty Design
Text design and composition by John Reinhardt Book Design

50 WAYS TO STAND UP FOR AMERICA
Copyright 2002 by Starburst Publishers, Inc.
All rights reserved.

First printing, April 2002
ISBN: 1-892016-70-2
Library of Congress Catalog Number: 2001099376
Printed in USA

Manuscript prepared by W. B. Freeman Concepts, Inc., Tulsa, Oklahoma.

Contents

III

INTRODUCTION Standing Up for What Is True and Precious

V

In the truest sense, freedom cannot be bestowed; it must be achieved.

—FRANKLIN D. ROOSEVELT

WHAT DOES IT MEAN to stand up for America? In some cases it means to speak up.

In some cases it means to give up or to yield a degree of cherished individualism in order to embrace the greater community that we call our nation. Those things that we give up, of course, are things that we are better for having yielded—generally speaking, a giving up of our self-centered pride and selfishness.

To give to one's country takes many forms—from enlisting in a branch of military service, to writing letters to one's congressman or senator, to helping those less fortunate, to caring for the physical land, to instilling patriotism in our children.

In virtually all cases, to stand up for America means to stand up on the inside—to take courage and to have faith that our nation's ills can be righted, our nation's wounds can be healed, and our nation's conflicts can be resolved.

Certainly to stand up for America means that we stand up for one another and embrace the fact that we are a nation of many cultures, ethnicities, religions, and dreams. To stand up for America also means that, in facing the world, we stand as a united people. While we may disagree on methodologies, we stand together in principle: All men and women are created with an inalienable right to live in equality before the law, to pursue liberty and justice within the rule of law, and to voice their opinions and beliefs without recrimination.

To stand up for America means to believe in one's heart that the United States of America is the greatest nation on earth and to believe that it can be even greater. To stand up means to *act* in a way that supports what we believe—to do the hard work necessary to build a great nation and to pass on a sense of responsibility for that work to the next generation. Patriotism is not only a feeling of the heart but also an act of the will that plays out in what we say and support with our time, energy, ideas, and money. Patriotism is something we *do*.

The fifty ideas presented in this book are all practical. They are things an average person can do—some to a greater degree than others, but nonetheless, all can participate. These are things that can be done with little expense, and in some cases, very few hours a month or year.

The fifty ideas are ones that can be done apart from a person's religious preferences, cultural background, or political persuasion. All that is required is a basic love for country and a desire to see the United States of America endure as "one nation, under God, indivisible, with liberty and justice for all."

If we do *not* stand up for America, the consequences are grim—we falter, become weak, or fail. If we do not believe in our greatness, we will not pursue it. If we do not speak what we believe, we will not encourage others to pursue greatness. If we do not enact what we speak, we will not achieve greatness.

This book is also a call to STAND UP! And even more, it is a declaration that the United States of America is *worth* standing up for.

—W. B. FREEMAN

Treat the Flag with Respect

1

Off with your hat, as the flag goes by! And let the heat have its say; you're man enough for a tear in your eye that you will not wipe away.

—HENRY CUYLER BUNNER

S TAND UP FOR AMERICA by standing up for the flag— literally! Some well-meaning people refuse to stand in honor of the flag passing because they fear their standing might border on idolatry or worship of an object. We do not *revere* the flag, however, as a sacred object. Rather, we respect the flag for what it represents—a nation of free people who retain the hard-won opportunity to live as they choose. Respectful behavior toward the flag is a demonstration of respect for those who have given their all, whether through life or death, to secure democratic freedom. Respectful behavior doesn't mean turning a blind eye to America's problems—it simply shows gratitude for our nation, imperfections and all.

A Uniting Symbol of Stars and Stripes

Our forefathers knew how important the flag would be as a symbol to help unite a diverse group of immigrants as one people. In 1775, the Continental Congress appointed a committee consisting of Benjamin Franklin, Benjamin Harrison, and Thomas Lynch to help design our nation's flag. The committee conferred with several Revolutionary War leaders including George Washington. It's important to remember that those fighting in the revolution wanted *freedom*, but not necessarily estrangement, from England. After all, most of those early leaders had family roots in England. Our flag also has English roots.

A small parish church in Great Brington, England, houses in its choir loft the tombstone of George Washington's great, great, great grandfather. The stone is recognizable because it bears the family crest, which General Washington later used on his personal stationery. The crest is instantly recognizable to Americans who are often astonished to see three stars over two bars.

While the stars and stripes now represent the thirteen original colonies and fifty states, they nevertheless pay silent respect to both George Washington and the patriots of our nation's founding.

Washington said this about the design of our flag: "We take the stars from heaven, the red from our mother country, separating it by white stripes, thus showing that we have separated from her, and the white stripes shall go down to posterity, representing our liberty."

Flag Ceremonies

Flag ceremonies remind us to honor those who have fought for our freedom. The flag-folding ceremony represents a number of the same religious principles on which our country was originally founded. Flags removed from display are folded thirteen times in a precise way. Traditionally these folds have specific meanings.

The first fold of our flag is a symbol of life.

The second fold is a symbol of our belief in eternal life.

The third fold is made in honor and remembrance of veterans who served to defend our nation and sought to attain peace throughout the world.

The fourth fold represents our weaker nature, for as American citizens trusting in God, it is to him we turn for divine guidance in times of peace as well as in times of war.

The fifth fold is a tribute to our nation. Stephen Decatur said, "Our country, in dealing with other countries, may she always be right; but it is still our country, right or wrong."

The sixth fold is for where our hearts lie. It is with our heart that we pledge allegiance to the flag of the United States of America, and to the republic for which it stands.

The seventh fold is a tribute to those who presently serve in our Armed Forces.

The eighth fold is a tribute to the ones who have entered into the valley of the shadow of death, that we might see the light of day, and to honor mothers (for whom it flies on Mother's Day).

The ninth fold is a tribute to womanhood; for it has been through women's faith, love, loyalty, and devotion that the character of those who have made this nation great has been molded.

The tenth fold is a tribute to fathers, for they, too, have given their sons and daughters for the defense of our nation.

The eleventh fold, in the eyes of a Hebrew citizen, represents the lower portion of the seal of King David and King

Solomon, and glorifies, in their eyes, the God of Abraham, Isaac, and Jacob.

The twelfth fold, in the eyes of a Christian citizen, represents an emblem of eternity and glorifies, in their eyes, God the Father, Son, and Holy Spirit.

When the flag is completely folded, the stars are uppermost, reminding us of our national motto, "In God We Trust." Folded and tucked in, it takes on the appearance of a cocked hat, reminding us of the soldiers who served under General George Washington and the sailors and marines who served under Captain John Paul Jones who were followed by their comrades and shipmates in the Armed Forces of the United States, preserving for us the rights, privileges, and freedoms we enjoy today.

2 Display a Flag with Pride

One flag, one land, one heart, one hand, one nation, evermore!

5

—OLIVER WENDELL HOLMES

PEOPLE IN EVERY NATION show their national pride by displaying their nation's flag. A flag is much more than just a piece of cloth. As a symbol, a national flag evokes strong sentiments of patriotism, courage, and even sacrifice. Because of the powerful symbolism of a flag, rules of etiquette have been developed for the proper display of our flag.

When to Fly the Flag

In the United States, the flag should be displayed every day except when weather conditions are severe enough to damage the flag. It is standard custom to display the flag only from sunrise to sunset on buildings or on permanent outdoor flagpoles. If a spotlight shines on the flag, however, it may be displayed twenty-four hours a day.

The flag should be flown on or near the main administration building of every public institution, in or near every school building during school days, and at polling places on election days. The flag should also be flown on federal public holidays: Martin Luther King Day, January 15; Presidential Inauguration Day, January 20 (every 4th year); Presidents' Day, February 22; Armed Forces Day, the third Saturday in May; Memorial Day, the last Monday in May; Flag Day, June 14; Independence Day, July 4; Labor Day, the first Monday in September; Citizenship Day, September 17; Columbus Day, the second Monday in October; and Veterans Day, November 11.

How to Display the Flag

When flags are displayed outdoors with the flags of other nations, each flag should be flown from a separate staff of equal height; the flags should be about the same size. The position of honor is reserved for the nation's own flag. In a display of flags on property of the United States of America, the flag of the United States should be hoisted first and lowered last. If the U.S. flag is flown on the same halyard with flags of a state or city, the U.S. flag should always be at the top.

When used on a speaker's platform, a flag hung on a staff should have a prominent place at the speaker's right but should not be used as decoration. Instead, bunting in the national colors can be used with the blue stripe displayed on the top. If the flag is displayed flat on a wall on a speaker's platform, it should be above and behind the speaker.

When raising and lowering a U.S. flag, the flag should be run up quickly and lowered slowly, and gathered and folded before it touches the ground.

Flying the Flag at Half-Staff

On presidential order, the flag is flown at half-staff on the death of principal government figures in respect to their memory. When a flag is flown at half-staff, the flag should first be hoisted briefly to the peak, and then lowered to the half-staff position. When flown at half-mast, the flag should be raised again to the peak before it is lowered for the day. On Memorial Day, the flag should be displayed at half-staff until noon, and then raised to the top of the staff.

At a Funeral

When the flag is used to cover a casket, it should be placed so that the union is at the head and over the left shoulder. The flag should not be lowered into the grave or allowed to touch the ground. It may be used again after the funeral.

In Processions

In a procession, the flag should be carried aloft to fly freely. It should not be dipped to any person or thing. State flags or regimental colors are to be dipped as a mark of honor. When a national flag is carried into a meeting hall, everyone in the hall should stand facing the platform. When a flag is raised or lowered as part of a ceremony, or when it passes by in a parade or in review, everyone should face it and stand at attention. Those present in military uniform should give a hand salute. Citizens not in military uniform should salute by placing their right hand over the heart; a man with a hat should remove it and hold it to his left shoulder, hand over the heart.

Wearing and Using the Flag

The flag should never be used as wearing apparel, bedding, or drapery. A flag patch may be attached to uniforms of firefighters or police officers. A flag lapel pin should be worn on the left lapel near the heart. The flag should never have placed upon it, nor attached to it, any mark, insignia, design, drawing, or picture. It should never be used for receiving, holding, carrying, or delivering anything.

 A national flag may be mended, dry cleaned, or washed. An old flag may be displayed as long as it is in respectable condition. When it is no longer fit for display, it should be destroyed in a dignified way, preferably by burning.

Citizens who love their nation also love the flag that represents it. The most important point in displaying a flag is to remember that our flag should be honored and handled with respect.

Teach Your Children the Pledge of Allegiance

3

The whole inspiration of our life as a nation flows out from the waving folds of this banner.

—ANONYMOUS

ONE OF OUR FOUNDING FATHERS, Thomas Jefferson, said this about teaching others the importance of civic responsibility: "I know of no safe depository of the ultimate powers of the society but the people themselves; and if we think them not enlightened enough to exercise their control with a wholesome discretion, the remedy is not to take it from them, but to inform their discretion." Certainly parents are among those entrusted to "inform" their children about patriotic duty!

Parents can both *take* opportunities and *make* opportunities to train their children in citizenship. One of the simple lessons that can be learned by a child at an early age is the Pledge of Allegiance. The Pledge was first written and published in 1892 for the four hundredth anniversary of Columbus' arrival in America. In its original form the pledge read:

> *I pledge allegiance to my Flag and to the Republic for which it stands: one Nation indivisible, with Liberty and Justice for all.*

The words "my flag" were replaced by "the flag of the United States" in 1923 for clarification in the aftermath of World War I. A year later, "of America" was added after "United States." No form of the pledge received official recognition by Congress until June 22, 1942, when it was formally included in the U.S. Flag Code. The official name of "The Pledge of Allegiance" was adopted in 1945. The last change in language came on Flag Day 1954, when Congress passed a law that added the words "under God" after "one nation."

The Pledge of Allegiance now reads:

> *I pledge allegiance to the flag of the United States of America and to the Republic for which it stands, one Nation under God, indivisible, with liberty and justice for all.*

Phrase by Phrase

As you teach your children the words of the Pledge, teach them also what each phrase means:

★ *I pledge allegiance* is a promise to be true and loyal.

★ *to the flag*—the flag is a symbol of our nation and it is recognized worldwide as a symbol of freedom.

★ *of the United States of America*—each state has joined with the other forty-nine states to be one country.

★ *and to the Republic for which it stands*—a republic is a nation in which individuals choose others to represent them in matters of government.

★ *one Nation*—the United States is a single nation.

★ *under God*—the nation recognizes dependence on and belief in a Supreme Being.

★ *indivisible*—the nation cannot be divided.

★ *with liberty*—the freedom of each individual to live one's own life

★ *and justice*—fairness.

★ *for all*—for each person in the nation.

Saluting While Reciting

Under the United States Code, Title 36, Chapter 10, Paragraph 172, the Pledge of Allegiance should be recited standing, facing the flag with the right hand over the heart. Persons in uniform should give the traditional hand-over-eyebrow military salute as they say the Pledge.

4

Beautify the Land

12

What makes a nation in the beginning is a good piece of geography.

—ROBERT FROST

AMERICA IS A NATION that is blessed with stunning natural beauty. Majestic mountain ranges, millions of acres of forestland, spectacular lakes, streams, and rivers—every part of our vast nation has unique natural beauty.

"America the Beautiful," one of the most loved patriotic songs of our nation, celebrates the extraordinary natural beauty of the physical land encompassed by the United States. The song was written by Katharine Lee Bates who was inspired to write it after viewing the mountains from the top of Colorado's Pike's Peak. The first verse, especially, speaks about the land:

> O beautiful for spacious skies,
> For amber waves of grain,
> For purple mountain majesties

Above the fruited plain!
America! America!
God shed his grace on thee
And crown thy good with brotherhood
From sea to shining sea!

Because of the vastness of our nation, it is easy to take areas of natural beauty for granted and assume they will always be there. But we know that's not true. Intentional effort is required to keep our nation clean and beautiful. And it takes cooperation—everyone taking responsibility for his or her own yard, neighborhood, and community.

If your community needs "beautifying," take the initiative to clean up, spruce up, and perk up—starting in your neighborhood. First, remove the litter. Second, plant trees, bushes, and flowers. Third, recruit volunteers to help.

Litter Removal

Pick up trash whenever you come across it. You might also coordinate or help with litter pickups of vacant lots and streets that are eyesores to the community. Help organize a cleanup campaign for cleaner streets, school yards, parks, and neighborhoods.

Encourage groups to take pride in their community by adopting a street, park, or other public area and keeping it litter-free, pest-free, and weed-free. As part of the cleanup campaign, distribute car litterbags to the public. Ask a local company to donate litterbags and then organize their distribution to the citizens of your town through your schools, retailers, and neighborhood associations.

Set up a time and place for citizens to turn in items and substances that cannot be disposed of through the local sanitation or refuse department. Car batteries, computer monitors, unused paint, and old oil cans that cannot be put in garbage pickup can be turned in and disposed of legally with the help of an environmental organization.

If you are posting signs—perhaps for a garage sale, a neighborhood picnic, or in support of a political candidate or issue—be sure to remove your own signs after the sale, picnic, or election. Don't expect others to clean up after you.

Beautification

This is the fun part—planting trees and flowers. Organize a group and focus your efforts on a neighborhood or public housing complex that needs landscaping or beautification. Ask local nurseries to donate trees or flowers, or contact the Department of Forestry or other agencies that distribute seedlings. Once a tree is planted be sure there is a plan in place to provide adequate watering until the young tree gets its roots established.

You might also plant a community flower garden as a community service project in public parks. Invite local garden clubs or horticultural societies to submit garden designs and flower suggestions, and ask for their expertise and assistance.

Some school campuses may be in need of beautification, too. Students take pride in their schools when the grounds are landscaped and well kept. Volunteers are also needed to help keep graffiti off the buildings. If playgrounds have become run-down or need work to repair or replace equipment, solicit neighborhood parents to provide leadership to help students bring the playground to new standards.

Organize a Neighborhood Cleanup Day through your school and give awards and publicity to the best-kept neighborhoods. Reward individual residents with "Best Kept Yard" awards.

Recruit Volunteers

Don't let neighborhood cleanup be an annual event—make it a routine practice. It is one challenge to get the initial cleanup and plantings done—and quite another to maintain the progress you made.

Maintenance can be best done through neighborhoods. Encourage the organization of neighborhood associations in each part of town to develop pride in keeping communities clean and beautiful.

A beautiful nation is a heritage, a trust to preserve and pass on to the next generation. Those who live in neighborhoods and areas that are physically attractive nearly always voice greater pride in the area where they live! What is true at the local level is also true at the national level.

Note: The lyrics for "America the Beautiful" can be found in appendix D.

5

Rediscover National Holidays

You have to love a nation that celebrates its independence every July 4, not with a parade of guns, tanks, and soldiers who file by the White House in a show of strength and muscle, but with family picnics where kids throw Frisbees, the potato salad gets iffy, and the flies die from happiness. You may think you have overeaten, but it is patriotism.

—ERMA BOMBECK

REDISCOVERING THE MEANING behind our national holidays and why they were originally celebrated can help you regain an understanding about how special it is to be an American. Below is a list of our major national holidays, why we celebrate these days or events, and some ideas that may help your family celebrate the true meaning of each day.

Solemn War-Related Holidays

A number of national holidays are days that commemorate our nation's struggle to become or remain free. These solemn holidays merit our doing things that help honor those who gave their lives in times of war:

★ *V-E Day* (May 8). Known as Victory in Europe day, it commemorates Germany's surrender in World War II, 1945. Fly your flag. Ask a WWII veteran to speak to your club, class, or other group.

★ *Memorial Day* (Last Monday in May). Formerly called Decoration Day, it has been observed since the Civil War. This day honors United States military personnel who died in wars. Fly your flag at half-mast, attend a ceremony, and place flowers or small flags at veterans' graves. Memorial Day is a legal holiday.

★ *Armed Forces Day* (Third Saturday in May). This is a day to honor all U.S. armed forces. Attend air shows or military displays in your area. Encourage your children to talk to the military hosts at displays and ask questions.

★ *D Day* (June 6). D Day marks the anniversary of the Allied troops' invasion of the Normandy region of France in 1944. This is also a good day to ask a WWII veteran to share his or her memories.

★ *Independence Day* (July 4). This legal holiday is the celebration of our Declaration of Independence from Great Britain. The Declaration was adopted by the Continental Congress in Philadelphia on this day in 1776. This is a great time to attend an outdoor concert. Take a picnic and stay for the evening fireworks. Discuss with your children how fireworks remind us of the war for independence.

★ *Veterans Day* (November 11). This anniversary of the signing of the armistice, which ended World War I in 1918, is a legal holiday. It should be celebrated with flags and singing of some of the old standards that came out of this war. Rent movies made before the mid to late 1930s to get a feeling of what life was like in America as it recovered from WWI.

★ *Pearl Harbor Day* (December 7). On this day in 1941, the Japanese launched a surprise attack on the U.S. Pacific Fleet at Pearl Harbor on Oahu Island, Hawaii, which was then a U.S. territory. The resulting action was the immediate entry of the United States into World War II. Approximately 2,400 Americans were killed and another 1,300 were injured. Eighteen ships were hit and approximately 200 aircraft were destroyed. Appropriate commemorations of this day include some of the following: Attend a special memorial service at your place of worship. Rent the 1942 movie, "Remember Pearl Harbor" and watch it with your family. Visit the memorial at Pearl Harbor if you visit Honolulu, Hawaii and take flowers to toss on the water over the sunken ships.

★ *Hiroshima Day* (August 6). On this day in 1945, the American bomber *Enola Gay* deployed the first atomic weapon used in wartime: A single bomb was dropped on the Japanese city of Hiroshima, destroying it completely. The action effectively ended WWII. Use this day to talk with your children about why wars must sometimes be fought. Discuss the use of nuclear weapons and become more aware of all the issues involved in nuclear disarmament.

★ *V-J Day* (August 14). This day commemorates the surrender of Japan, ending World War II in 1945.

Joyful Holidays

These holidays are joyful—they appropriately include prominent displays of flags and red, white, and blue crepe paper or bunting.

★ *Flag Day* (June 14). In 1949 Congress designated this day as national Flag Day. It commemorated adoption by the Continental Congress in 1777 of the Stars and Stripes as the national flag. Some schools observe the day with instruction in flag etiquette and flag-raising ceremonies.

★ *Inauguration Day* (January 20, every fourth year). This day begins the term of a newly-elected president and occurs every four years. Read or watch the president's inauguration speech and have a family discussion about it.

★ *Martin Luther King Jr. Birthday* (Third Monday in January). This legal holiday is set aside in the United States to honor the memory of the famed civil rights leader. Born on January 15, 1929, in Atlanta, Georgia, King fought segregation through the 1950s and 1960s. This day is used to reflect on issues of civil rights and racial equality.

★ *President's Day* (Third Monday in February). This day observes the birthdays of George Washington and Abraham Lincoln, and is a legal holiday. Have a "George and Abe" party and create a trivia game built around their presidencies.

★ *Labor Day* (First Monday in September). Labor Day honors working people and celebrates their history and accomplishments. It was initiated in 1882 by the Knights of Labor. First observed in New York City on Sept. 5, 1882, Labor Day is a legal holiday. Write short thank-you notes to two or three people who regularly perform services for you (the paperboy, dry cleaner, physician, beautician) and tell them that you appreciate their work. Tip waiters, doormen, bellhops, and others a little extra on this day.

★ *Citizenship Day* (September 17). Congress established this day in 1952 to give recognition to people who became American citizens in the preceding year. Visit Ellis Island (off Manhattan Island in New York) in person or virtually on the web. Research your own family roots to find out when your first ancestor set foot on American soil. Consider attending a citizenship ceremony if one is being held in your community.

★ *Columbus Day* (Second Monday in October). Also known as Discovery Day, this is the day we celebrate the landing of Christopher Columbus at San Salvador in 1492. This legal holiday is a good time to "discover" something new in your world. Try a new dish, meet a new friend, visit a new city, or go to an exhibit you haven't seen.

20 ## Some Lesser-Known National Holidays

Other national holidays that we recognize include the following:

★ *Emancipation Day* (June 20). Although President Lincoln declared all slaves free on January 1, 1863, this day officially observes the end of slavery in the United States. Watch the movie *Roots* with your family.

★ *Police Memorial Day* (May 15). This is the day to honor police killed while on duty. Write a letter of appreciation to your local police precinct.

★ *General Election Day* (First Tuesday after first Monday in November). This is the day to vote for elected officials. Presidential elections are held on years evenly divisible by four. House of Representatives elections and elections for a rotating third of senators are on even numbered years. Vote!

★ *Forefathers' Day* (December 21). This is the anniversary of the landing of the *Mayflower* at Plymouth in 1620. Read about the *Mayflower* and the first settlers.

Vote

6

The ballot is stronger than the bullet.

—ABRAHAM LINCOLN

21

THE MOST IMPORTANT RIGHT and responsibility of the citizens of a free nation is to vote. Voting is the key to democracy, the most basic means by which Americans participate in their government. Every person's vote counts the same as another person's vote.

Universal suffrage—the right of all adult citizens to vote—has not always existed in the United States. In 1789, the right to vote was granted only to white, adult, male property owners. Only about one out of every fifteen citizens qualified.

As various groups sought to gain the privilege of voting over the next two hundred years, the argument was nearly always couched in terms of "all citizens" having the right to vote. In advocating voting rights for women, Elizabeth Cady Stanton said, "Our 'pathway' is straight to the ballot box, with no variableness nor shadow of turning. . . . We demand in the Reconstruction suffrage for all the citizens of the Republic. I would not talk of Negroes or women, but of citizens."

Today, voting is the right of every citizen regardless of race, gender, or color, and at least eighteen years of age. A person convicted of a felony offense can lose the right to vote.

Registration

The first step toward becoming a voter is to register to vote. The purpose of voter registration is to avoid election fraud by identifying voters. A voter must register his or her name, place of residence, date of birth, and other pertinent information with an election official in his or her community. Usually, there is a residence requirement that the citizen must meet before that person can vote in that state. When a voter moves his residence, he must register again in his new precinct. If a voter is going to be out of town on Election Day, he needs to contact his election officials in advance to determine how to get an absentee ballot.

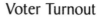

Voter Turnout

All elections are important. If citizens of a nation neglect their responsibility to vote, they may eventually find that they have lost that right. National elections for president and U.S. Congress naturally generate greater interest and get a higher voter turnout than local elections, but it's important that citizens vote in every election.

Elections decide a vast number of issues: school matters such as passing bond issues and choosing school board members; local referendum that impact taxes and use of tax monies; and selection of city, county, and state representatives; and some judicial issues. Officials can be voted in or out of office and proposals can be defeated or passed by your vote. Make voting a habit—vote every time the polls are open!

Voter Information

Freedom of speech and freedom of information are vital to a free society and to an effective "vote."

Where can a voter get good information? The League of Women Voters and Voter Information Services are two of the best known groups that work to provide voters with accurate, fair, and comprehensive information. Try to get a copy of a sample ballot to read the issues and names of candidates so you will know what you are voting on before you enter the voting booth. Ballots are often printed in the local newspaper prior to the election.

Hear All Sides

It's important that voters read and hear a variety of sources in making their decisions to vote. Read the editorials and op-ed pages in your local newspaper. Listen to debates on television. Watch several different news programs to try to get a balanced perspective of the candidates and issues. Local elections often feature live debates for voters to attend to hear the candidates address issues.

Find out what special interest groups endorse a candidate and who is donating to the campaign election costs. That will tell you a lot about whether or not your sympathies are with that candidate. You can also contact an elected official to find out where he or she stands on issues, and why.

Discuss Elections with Your Children

Discuss upcoming elections with your children to encourage provocative, thoughtful consideration of issues and candidates. Ask your children how they would vote in an upcoming election and why they would vote that way. Encourage them to find ways to get information about issues. You may even stage a debate with the children taking opposite sides so they can appreciate the arguments and complexities involved in political decision making.

7 Host an Exchange Student

24

America cannot be an ostrich with its head in the sand.

—WOODROW WILSON

HOSTING AN EXCHANGE STUDENT can be a wonderful way to help build bridges of understanding between the United States and other countries. If the testimonials of previous hosts are any measure, the experience can change your life in positive ways you may never have thought possible.

The word "exchange" does not imply that you or another family must send your teenager abroad. It refers to the exchange of ideas, cultural understanding, and language skills that occur among the student, his or her host family, and the host family's community.

Taking a high school exchange student into your home brings international relations down to the person-to-person level. Many host families feel as though their student becomes a full member of their families, and they often remain in contact with the student for many years after the student returns to his home country.

Students and hosts alike have the opportunity to improve their foreign language skills and to learn about another culture. "I loved learning about another culture and how people do things," one host said. "I believe I made a difference in a teenager's life and that is a pretty awesome thing. And, I think I helped someone see some of the good in America."

Host Families

Host families come in many shapes and sizes. They may be families with teens or no children at all. They might be empty nesters, single parents, or grandparents. Host families live in large cities, suburban areas, on farms and ranches, or in small communities. The one thing you must have is the willingness to open your home to a student for up to one year and to take responsibility for him or her as American host and "parent" (although the student's natural parents remain legal guardians).

Typically, exchange students must agree to participate in the life of the family, which includes going on family trips, attending your place of worship, and abiding by the basic rules of conduct expected in the family. Students are usually "cream of the crop" young people; they are adventuresome and eager to take on new experiences. School attendance is, of course, a critical part of the student's experience, so the host parent can expect to participate in some school activities. Students come with their own money for most expenses. Volunteer American host families provide students with a place to sleep, meals, and a loving, supportive home life. Students are allowed to share a bedroom with the host family's teen of the same sex, but the student must have his or her own bed.

Hosts are not paid but may deduct $50 a month as a charitable contribution from their itemized tax returns for hosting a foreign exchange student. (The proper supporting documentation is available from the host organization.) In reality, hosts, like other parents, often find themselves supplementing the expenses of their student in small ways, but they should never feel obligated to take on bigger expenses such as airfare or special clothing (such as prom dresses or tuxedos).

Hosts are usually asked to refrain from trying to change someone's religion, but they are encouraged to include the student in all aspects of family activity.

Applicants

Each potential host family must fill out an application form, which provides a detailed summary and profile of the family. Families are usually screened by the hosting organization in an in-home interview with all members of the family present. Applicants must also provide personal references from members of their community or school attesting to their good character.

The students are equally well screened and most host organizations attempt to match the preferences expressed by both host and student as to which countries are involved, family and city sizes, and sex of the student. Some organizations actually allow the host family to choose the student. Students usually have a minimum of three years of English instruction and have passed an English language proficiency test to qualify them as having a working knowledge of the English language.

Before your student arrives, take time to learn about the culture from which they are coming. This is especially important if the student is coming here from an Asian, Arab, African, or other culture that differs greatly from American culture.

26

Talk about these differences with other family members. Discuss ways to help the new member feel at home and ways to help him or her become integrated into American society and your home. This will ease the transition for both your family and the student.

Getting Started

How do you get started? There are a number of nonprofit organizations that arrange foreign exchanges. Three such organizations are listed below. First, check with your local high school; you are likely to receive more support and be able to meet previous hosts if there is a program already active in your school. You may also obtain information from your local Rotary International chapter.

1. The American Intercultural Student Exchange (AISE)
   7720 Herschel Avenue
   La Jolla, California 92037
   Phone: (858) 459-9761
   Toll Free info line 1-800-SIBLINGFAX (858) 459-5301
   http://www.aise.com/

2. AYUSA International
   2226 Bush Street
   San Francisco, CA 94115
   Phone: (888) 55-AYUSA
   Fax: (415) 674-5232
   http://www.ayusa.org/

3. EF Foundation for Foreign Study
   EF Center Boston
   One Education Street
   Cambridge MA 02141
   Phone: 1-800-44-SHARE
   Email: EFFoundation@ef.com

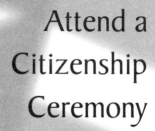

8

Attend a Citizenship Ceremony

28

It is the flag just as much of the man who was naturalized yesterday as of the men whose people have been here many generations.

—HENRY CABOT LODGE

CITIZENSHIP SWEARING-IN CEREMONIES remind us of what a wonderful gift we received if we were born on U.S. soil. Ceremonies are held across the nation in local communities throughout the year, but those held on national holidays are likely to deliver double-dose shots of patriotism for those who attend.

Attending a swearing-in ceremony is an excellent way to help children (and adults!) of all ages begin to understand what being a citizen of the United States really means.

Finding a Citizenship Swearing-In Ceremony

Swearing in new citizens is the job of federal district courts although the ceremonies themselves may be held in a variety of venues and may be hosted by various civil organizations such as a Boy Scout troop or the VFW (Veterans of Foreign Wars). To find out where and when ceremonies in your area will be held, call the federal district judge's office in your area (listed in the federal government section of your phone book). You might also want to inquire how your club or organization can host a ceremony.

What to Do before You Go

Immigrants wishing to become citizens must first work their way through a maze of paperwork and tests in order to become naturalized citizens. Many citizens born and educated in the United States would probably have a hard time passing the test. You can make the ceremony a rich experience for you and your family or group if you do one or more of the following:

★ Read newspaper articles focusing on ethnic and immigrant communities in your area to get a sense of the ethnic groups from which the new naturalized citizens may come. Find out what is happening in the nations from which they have emigrated. Learn about the hardships the new citizens may be leaving behind.

★ Ask Immigration and Naturalization Services to send you materials sent to prospective citizens. Call 1-800-870-3676 and request the N-400 forms. Included with the forms is a question-and-answer booklet about becoming a U.S. citizen.

★ Take a sample citizenship test in appendix F. Consider making up your own Trivial Pursuit or Academic Bowl game using questions from the citizenship test.

★ Pick up a bouquet of inexpensive flowers or tiny American flags to hand to the new citizens at the end of the ceremony.

Attending the Ceremony

This is a special occasion for the new citizens as well as for their friends and family. Honor the occasion by wearing business attire. Wear your uniform if you are in the armed forces or belong to a civic club that has a uniform such as the Boy Scouts or Girl Scouts.

Most ceremonies will be brief, but some, hosted by Scouts or other civic groups, might feature a color guard or flag ceremony. Others might include some music. Prominent elected officials are likely to offer the official welcome.

Some new citizens will change their names to a more pronounceable or Americanized form during the ceremony. Make a note of these new names so that you can be among the first to use that new name when you congratulate them after the ceremony. "Allow me to be among the first to welcome you as a fellow citizen, Mr. _____!" might bring you the biggest smile you've seen in a while!

The Oath of Allegiance

The oath of allegiance is the centerpiece of the citizenship swearing-in ceremony.

OATH OF ALLEGIANCE

I hereby declare, on oath, that I absolutely and entirely renounce and abjure all allegiance and fidelity to any foreign prince, potentate, state or sovereignty of whom or which I have heretofore been a subject or citizen; that I will support and defend the constitution and the laws of the United States of America against all enemies, foreign and domestic; that I will bear true faith and allegiance to the same; that I will bear arms on behalf of the

30

United States when required by the law; that I will per-
form noncombatant service in the Armed Forces of the
United States when required by the law; that I will per-
form work of national importance under civilian direc-
tion when required by the law; and that I take this
obligation freely without any mental reservation or pur-
pose of evasion: SO HELP ME GOD.

You can find out more about what it takes to become a naturalized citizen of the United States by visiting this web site: http://www.ins.usdoj.gov.

Note: A sample citizenship test and answers are found in appendix F.

9 Befriend New Immigrants

32

Here [in America] individuals of all nations are melted into a new race of men.

—MICHEL GUILLAUME JEAN DE CREVECOEUR

IMAGINE MOVING TO A NEW NEIGHBORHOOD with strange customs and a difficult language. Even though opportunity and possibilities for a better life brought you to this place, the transition needs one important ingredient—a friend.

Immigrants who have obtained a status that allows them to work or study here may not be prepared for life in your community. Often they have a support community of others from their home country who are also either resident aliens or new citizens. While these associations may provide a network of people who can help with basic orientation skills, they can also be isolating. If a newcomer relies solely on his own ethnic group for all social interaction, his opportunities for full involvement in the American culture are likely to be stunted.

Official Sponsorship

The U.S. government receives thousands of immigration requests from refugee families fleeing persecution in their homelands. Before these refugees are allowed to enter our nation, however, a person or organization must agree to be their sponsor. By and large, refugee families come here at great personal cost with little money, little or no English, and no family or friends in the United States. Sponsorship means helping the family find shelter, jobs, and a way of acquiring basic English skills. Many churches, synagogues, and civic organizations have become sponsors with their members sharing the duties to help a family settle.

33

Getting Involved

Even if you do not belong to an organization that sponsors or works with refugees and immigrants, you can still get involved in these ways:

★ Contact your local ministerial alliance to find out if local congregations in your area are sponsoring immigrant families or refugees. Volunteer to help teach English as a second language, provide rides to work, baby-sit children after school until the immigrant parents get off work, or even take the family to a special concert or museum in your area to help introduce them to their new hometown.

★ Explore ways to start such a project in your house of worship or civic organization.

★ Call your city government to find out how to contact immigrant support groups in your area.

★ Visit the pastor of a place of worship where services are conducted in another language and ask how you can help new immigrants in the congregation.

★ Foster a sister-congregation relationship between your place of worship and the immigrant congregation.

★ Organize a Transition Closet to provide clothes for new-comers who need clothing for job interviews or dressier work settings. Encourage donations of gently worn clothing.

★ Host a party featuring the foods and customs of the immigrant family and ask them to help you put it together.

★ Invite neighbors and other people who haven't met the immigrant family to come to your home for dinner or a welcome tea.

34

★ Host a citizen's shower for a refugee family who is moving into their own apartment or home.

★ Tutor a would-be citizen in preparation for the citizenship test.

★ Take a new immigrant on a day trip to a nearby area or town that will help him or her see the diversity of our nation.

★ Include new immigrant friends in your holiday celebrations with family and friends.

★ Invite new friends to sing, dance, or speak to your place of worship or civic group.

★ Help a new immigrant find a job—perhaps with your company. If he or she is hired, stop by the work location every few days for the first month to see how things are going.

10 Support Your Local Schools

Next in importance to freedom and justice is popular education, without which neither freedom nor justice can be permanently maintained.

—JAMES GARFIELD

S CHOOLS GET BETTER when educators and families work together. And better schools make for better students, and, in turn, better citizens.

Start at Home

Family attitudes toward education are the most important ingredient in a child's success at school. Students who come from families that value education do better in school. There are many ways a family communicates education as a priority:

★ Read together at home. Children who read at home with their parents perform better in school. As a parent, keep good books, magazines, and newspapers in your home and model good reading habits. Regularly check out books from your local library and discuss the books you read with your children.

★ Limit the use of television. Academic achievement drops when children watch more than two hours of television a day. Help your child select educational programs to watch and limit your child's total amount of television viewing time.

★ Establish family routines that support homework time and regular school attendance. Set aside a place for children to study that is quiet and well lit.

★ Talk to your children and teenagers and listen to them. Initiate conversations with your children about the dangers of drugs and alcohol and be intentional about teaching them the values you want them to learn.

★ Express high expectations for your children by enrolling them in challenging courses that require hard work. Most children *like* to be challenged to learn something that is difficult, and which a parent believes the child can master.

★ Stay informed about your children's progress at school. Get to know the names of teachers, principals, and counselors. Visit with your child's teachers in person or on the telephone.

What Communities Can Do

Communities that have good schools and better-educated residents are almost always safer, more stable communities where businesses and families thrive.

★ Create school-family-community partnerships. Parents, community residents, and law enforcement officials might join together in creating voluntary organizations and neighborhood watches to resolve safety problems. School, community, and religious organizations can unite to offer after-school cultural and recreational activities.

★ Combat alcohol, drugs, and violence that threaten children's health and well-being. Prevention programs work best with a combined effort by parents, students, schools, law enforcement officials, and communities. Provide mentoring and after-school programs.

★ Offer high-quality parenting skills programs to young and new parents to help in the critical years of child development. Programs for parents might include literacy training, career preparation, early childhood education, children's health, and assistance in finding helpful services in the community.

★ Provide mentoring programs to provide emotional support and guidance to young people. Mentors can help with schoolwork, job skill development, and career planning.

★ Enlist community volunteers as tutors, teacher aides, library workers, and school crossing guards.

★ Offer summer learning programs through schools, recreation centers, science and art museums, libraries, and parks. These are particularly important for students with limited access to books and computers at home.

★ Support preschool programs to help improve children's achievements and adjustments to school.

You can find many ways to support public schools, and many groups within the schools will welcome your interest. A phone call to your local school or volunteering an hour of your time can be the first step.

11 Get to Know Your Neighbors

There is no power on earth equal to the power of free men and women united in the bonds of human brotherhood.

—WALTER P. REUTHER

D O YOU KNOW YOUR nearest neighbors? If you are like millions of Americans, you don't. In a mobile society and in a society in which all people in a household tend to work, study, or engage in recreation away from the home, many people cannot name more than two people who live adjacent to them—next door, across the street, or across the alley. Generally, those who can name two or more neighbors do not know their neighbor's last names or anything about their personal or professional lives.

One of the foremost ways to build a sense of community and patriotic pride is to get to know your neighbors. This is also an excellent way to increase the security of your neighborhood.

Greet Your Neighbors

If you feel reluctant to go next door to introduce yourself after you have lived adjacent to a person or family for months—even years—find an excuse for ringing that doorbell. The holiday season is a prime opportunity. Any holiday will do! Take over a small, inexpensive gift—perhaps even that proverbial welcome-to-the-neighborhood cake or loaf of bread that you had intended to bake but never did—and admit, "I haven't been a very good neighbor. I at least want to introduce myself." If you know the person next door enjoys gardening or decorating for a holiday, your gift could be something in keeping with their interest. If you have gathered from observation that the person travels a great deal, your gift could be a "certificate" of neighborly help—for example, one free mowing of their front yard or picking up their newspaper the next time they go on vacation.

Become an "Alert Neighborhood"

If you feel reluctant to make the first move, you may find that the mayor's office—or perhaps a local fire station or police precinct—can be a valuable ally. Most cities have "Alert Neighborhood" programs. Neighbors are invited to a central location—a community center, home, park—for a meeting to discuss ways to prevent crime. The meetings provide valuable practical information, as well as a good neutral setting in which neighbors can get to know one another.

Hold a Neighborhood Party

Block parties can sometimes be organized with the help of a mayor's office or a homeowners association. But you can certainly have your own party. One homeowner decided that inviting the entire neighborhood would be too complicated and expensive, so he and his wife invited their adjacent neighbors—those who lived on either side and the family across the street—to a "deck party" in early fall. Flowers were at their peak in their patio, the aroma of hamburgers and hot dogs filled the air, and neighbors were asked only to bring their choice of beverage and their favorite CD of music. In a casual backyard atmosphere these neighbors got to know one another as their children played croquet.

 As part of the evening, the host and hostess challenged those present to "pass on" the invitation to *their* adjacent neighbors. Such a plan, of course, meant that the host and hostess themselves offered to participate and even help with food for the three parties held by their guests. The plan made it easier for the other families to break the ice as they reached out to those who lived on the other side of them or, in the case of the family across the street, both sides of their home. Over the course of the summer, clusters of four families met until everybody in the immediate housing development had been invited to at least four backyard parties!

Get to Know the Parents of Your Child's Friends

Children have a way of scouting out other children their own age in a neighborhood. Ride their coattails! Suggest to the parents of these children that you get together for an outing to a local zoo or nearby playground. The children will see it as a treat and you and the other parents will find this to be an easy way to get better acquainted without feeling that you need to invite the neighbors into your home.

Start a Neighborhood Newsletter

Consider challenging your older children and teens to write

and distribute a neighborhood newsletter. It may be only one page (one-sided or two-sided), perhaps distributed once a month or once a quarter. The newsletter can spotlight one or two families an issue, giving information about the names of those who live at an address, their family interests, the names of family pets, the ages of children, and so forth. Families that are profiled, of course, should give permission for this information to be distributed.

A neighborhood newsletter is also a good forum for advertising upcoming garage sales, the availability of teenagers to baby-sit, house-sit, mow lawns, rake leaves, walk pets, or help with other odd jobs, or provide information about the skills of retired adults in the neighborhood who may be willing to help with minor home maintenance or house-watching chores (for a fee or as a volunteer). Newsletters are also a good way of alerting all in a neighborhood to the opportunity to start a Scout troop, participate in a crime-prevention meeting, or help organize a neighborhood-wide patriotic parade or party.

The more you get to know your neighbors, the less likely your neighborhood is going to become a haven for would-be terrorists or criminals. The three things that both terrorists and criminals fear the most are eyes that see them, ears that hear them, and people who know their names.

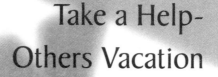

12 Take a Help-Others Vacation

There is nothing wrong with America that together we can't fix.

—RONALD REAGAN

ONE THING THAT AMERICANS do better than any other country in the world is give. We are philanthropic both as a nation and as individuals. We give more personal time, money, and goods of all varieties to worthy causes than any other people. We give at home and we give abroad. The paradox is that there are still many Americans who lack the basic necessities of life and who do not possess the basic skills they need to better their lot in life.

If America is the "Land of Opportunity," why are there so many adults who can't read and why are so many people living in tenements, houses in bad repair, or on the streets? And how can one person with limited resources change any of these problems?

The answer lies at the heart of why no other nation matches our level of philanthropy. By and large we have

42

learned that "to whom much is given, much is required." Put more simply, people who receive help are encouraged to help others. The pass-it-on principle is the answer to helping many who are struggling with poverty or who are living in need.

Getting Involved

Begin by talking with people around you—your family, closest buddies, or others with whom you spend your holidays and days off. Talk about the organizations in your area that use volunteers to help people get on their feet. Explore the talents within your group and discuss the kinds of things that you could do together during a holiday break and that would call upon your collective talents.

Don't plan your first "mission" together as a long-distance, multi-day commitment. Instead, choose a time when you have a one- or two-day vacation. Call a local shelter, place of worship, Salvation Army, food pantry, or other organization to volunteer your group to help with activities such as these:

★ Cook and serve Thanksgiving or Christmas dinner
★ Deliver baskets of food to families
★ Collect or deliver Christmas toys
★ Provide entertainment or lead in a carol singing

Doing these projects together with people you care about helps create a comradeship and eases the discomfort that some people feel when dealing with strangers.

A Volunteer Vacation Trip

There are many places that need your help. Is your place of worship planning a mission trip to help build or renovate a structure or tutor children in Appalachia, on a reservation, or in the inner city? If not, you can help plan such a trip. Begin planning your trip six to eight months in advance. Coordinate with other houses of worship and organizations who are already working in the area of your interest. Plan work groups that supplement or fill in gaps for the work that is already being done. Here are some activities to consider:

★ Tutor children or adults in math or reading skills

★ Help organize a free dental or pregnancy clinic and help pick up and deliver patients who need services

★ Help renovate or build housing, schools, or places of worship

★ Help collect books and educational materials, clothing, and household goods. Fill a trailer and deliver the goods during your vacation.

Beware: Volunteering vacations can be positive, life-changing experiences, especially for teens and young adults!

Put Your Personal and Professional Skills to Use

Does your employer or civic organization sponsor a nonprofit agency that is providing services to people in your city or a nearby area? Are you a health professional who could join a team headed to a disaster area to provide temporary services and relief?

Volunteering vacations are a good place to put an avocation or hobby to use. If you're a dentist with a knack for plumbing, an attorney who draws delightful cartoons and loves kids, a mechanic who enjoys acting and drama—there's a volunteer spot for you. Look in the yellow pages of your phone book under "volunteer" to see if there is a volunteer matching organization in your area. If not, you can get started by logging on to the following web site: http://www.volunteermatch.org. You will find opportunities to volunteer for an hour or a week as well as contacts and information about a volunteering vacation.

Working Together

Many excellent nonprofit organizations throughout the United States would value your volunteer efforts! If you see a problem or challenge that moves you to action, begin by seeking out others who have already begun working on that problem. Volunteer to help them. Nonprofit organizations need volunteers to deliver donated items, help in their offices, work with clients, raise funds, serve on their boards and help define their mission, and engage in dozens of other tasks.

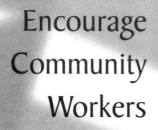

13

Encourage Community Workers

America is a willingness of the heart.

—F. SCOTT FITZGERALD

COUNTLESS PEOPLE IN ANY COMMUNITY must work sometimes twenty-four hours a day, seven days a week during times of crisis as well as on holidays. One of the most patriotic things a person can do is to encourage those who are working for the common good while the rest of us are working for our personal benefit or are relaxing with family and friends.

Crisis Workers

Both paid and unpaid volunteer workers need special encouragement in times of crisis. The crisis may be the damage caused by a natural disaster, such as a flood, tornado, or hurricane. The crisis may be caused by an accident, such as a plane crash or train wreck. Or it may be caused by a terrorist attack or war. To a great extent, the encouragement needed is dictated by the nature of the crisis:

★ Those working in cold or wet environments will be encouraged at the arrival of an armload of dry towels, a couple of blankets, a bundle of heavy-duty socks, or a pair of rubber boots. They will also enjoy jugs of hot soup, coffee, or hot chocolate.

★ Those working in environments where fire or collapsed buildings are involved will be encouraged by new steel-tipped shoes.

★ Those working to assist people who are injured will be encouraged by the arrival of clean clothing.

★ Those battling any large-scale tragedy are nearly always encouraged to see people who say simply, "Here are two more hands to do whatever you ask them to do, and two more feet (and possibly a vehicle) to go where you need me to go."

Workers are also encouraged when others help the *victims* they are assisting. The arrival of people willing to lend a listening ear, a warm touch, smile, prayer, and a comforting word is nearly always welcome.

A word of caution: Upon arrival at the scene of a crisis, make certain that you are more help than hindrance. Don't stand idly by and gawk. Find a person in authority and ask what you might do to help. If the person says no help is needed, back away. Don't intrude where help is not wanted or needed.

Holiday Workers

Firefighters, police, nurses, and other hospital workers, and a wide variety of other community workers are at their posts every holiday. Join with family members, friends, or your civic group to provide encouragement for these workers on holidays:

★ Take a gift of food. This need not be homemade. You might pick up a couple of pies from a local bakery or a tub of ice cream from a local store. Stop by the local firehouse, hospital, or police station with your gift a couple of hours *before* lunch or dinner. That will give those at the site an opportunity to make the most of your gift.

★ Give a gift of entertainment. Go caroling at Christmas. Get a comedy skit together and perform for the *staff* at the nursing home. Organize a musical ensemble. Extend the cheer of the holiday to those unable to participate in the celebration of their choice.

Comedian Bob Hope once said, "If I have to lay an egg for my country, I'll do it." Be creative in what you do to bring humor and good will to those who are working on holidays. Costumes, balloons, and unusual props can go a long way to make an event more memorable.

Be sure to keep your appearance brief. Staff in hospitals are *at work*. Those at volunteer crisis centers or at police and fire stations are *at work*. A ten-minute interruption can usually be accommodated, but a longer stay can be intrusive.

Letters of Encouragement

A letter of appreciation is always welcomed by community workers. You can write a letter personally or collectively as a family. You may want to put together a neighborhood letter—have your children or teens go door-to-door to get every person in your neighborhood to sign a big thank-you card. Then take it to the nearest fire station or police precinct.

You may want to encourage a school, Scout, youth center, or worship-related class to put together a "blessing jar" or create a "chain of good wishes." The idea here is to write one-line or one-word blessings, such as love, joy, peace, health on slips of paper or on paper chain links. Fill a jar with the blessings or link the strips of paper together to make a paper chain. Then take the jar or paper chain to a group of community workers and encourage them to read one link of the chain or pull one blessing from the jar anytime they are feeling lonely, discouraged, or disappointed.

Your note of encouragement need not be lengthy. Simply use one of the following ideas:

★ I'm aware that you are working on a day when most other people in our nation are not.

★ I'm thankful for the services you provide—I feel safer, more at peace, and more confident as a result of your work.

★ I value the profession you have chosen.

★ I wish you joy.

If you feel inclined, you may want to add "God bless you" or "I'm praying for you today."

14 Write to Your Elected Officials

We know the best way to enhance freedom in other lands is to demonstrate here that our democratic system is worthy of emulation.

—JIMMY CARTER

MOST OF US HAVE BEEN TOLD repeatedly, "Write to your elected representatives about this issue." Now is the time to follow through and *write*! The only way your elected representatives *truly* discover what you think as a citizen is for you to contact them and express your opinions, offer suggestions, give voice to your good ideas, and, perhaps most importantly, extend a word of appreciation or approval.

A Positive Word

Most elected officials get a predominance of mail that voices opposition or criticism. Few receive letters of congratulation, appreciation, or applause. When your elected representative takes a stand that you find courageous or bold, let him or her know. When your elected representative is given an honor or an award, count that as an opportunity for saying "way to go." If you see that a family member of an elected representative has won a special honor, take the time to jot a quick note that says, "You must be very pleased."

Elected representatives are people who mourn and suffer loss just as their constituents do. If you read a notice that a family member of an elected official has died, send a sympathy card.

Most elected officials, regardless of their personal religious preferences, appreciate receiving word from their constituents that conveys, "I am praying for you," "I am believing that God will impart to you wisdom and understanding," or "I am trusting God to reward your courageous stand."

Elected representatives take note of those who write positive messages to them. A string of positive messages in your correspondence file can make your occasional suggestion or opinion note all that more valued.

The Letter That Gets Read

In writing to an elected official, these simple and practical suggestions should be observed:

★ Keep your letter short. Do not exceed one page, and preferably, keep your letter to one or two short paragraphs.

★ Get to the point quickly. Reference your concern at the outset. For example, "I am writing to you in regard to House Bill #___" or "I am writing to you about an issue of great concern to me." Then state the issue succinctly.

★ Avoid rehearsing history. Speak in the present. Your elected official wants to know what you believe should be done *now*, not what you think should have been done last year, a decade ago, or in a previous century.

★ Be as practical as possible. If you have an idea or suggestion to offer, do so, but make sure the idea is stated in concrete terms—who would be involved, what the idea would cost, how the idea might be implemented, when the idea should be enacted, and what the expected outcomes might be.

★ Avoid any personal attacks or innuendos.

★ Sign your letter and give your address, phone number, and email address. This is especially important if you are offering an idea or suggestion, and not merely an opinion. Your home address also gives your elected official confirmation that you are from his or her area of representation. While "blanket" messages to all elected officials may be appropriate from time to time, specific messages to *your* elected representatives are always going to be taken more seriously and given more time and attention.

How to Communicate

If the legislation is pending or the timing of a situation is critical, call the office of your elected official. In all likelihood, your call will be answered by an aide, perhaps even a student intern. Be polite and succinct in your call. State your name and your "vote" on the matter, for example: "My name is Bill Smith. I live in district one. I am calling to voice an opinion about the upcoming House vote. I hope the congressman will vote yes (or no)."

Email messages are also welcomed by elected officials. Again, keep your message succinct. It's a good idea to include your address (not only your email address) as part of your memo.

Letters take longer to process so if time is a factor, call or send an electronic message.

If you need the address or email address for your elected

representative, you can find it on http://www.info.gov. Separate listings are also available for the U.S. Senate and U.S. House of Representatives. The toll-free number is 800-688-9889.

Your local phone directory is also likely to list the names, addresses, phone numbers, or email addresses of your federal representatives (senators and representatives), as well as information about your state, county, and city officials.

53

15 Be Kind to Your Mail Carrier

Freedom is still expensive. It still costs money. It still costs blood. It still calls for courage and endurance, not only in soldiers, but in every man and woman who is free and who is determined to remain free.

—HARRY S. TRUMAN

UNTIL RECENT DAYS, few Americans were likely to think of postal workers as being courageous, but in the wake of a series of anthrax-related terrorist attacks launched through the U.S. Postal Service, all postal workers have taken on an added risk as part of their government jobs.

There are several things you can do to encourage your local postal workers:

★ If a mail carrier comes to your door with a package, greet him or her with a smile and say, "Thank you for the service you give to our country."

★ Don't grumble as you stand in line at the local post office. Be pleasant to the clerks who serve you.

★ Make sure your dog is kept in a fenced or other secure area so your mail carrier can deliver your mail without fear of being bitten.

★ Leave a note in your outgoing mail addressed to "My Postal Carrier." Express your appreciation that he or she delivers your mail in rain, snow, sleet, or shine.

★ Keep bushes—especially prickly or thorny ones—trimmed away from your mailbox for easier delivery and no-scratch access by postal vehicles.

★ Address your mail clearly and accurately. You'll help remove some of the stress in your local post office.

★ Remember your mail carrier at Christmas with a small gift—perhaps a small box of chocolates or other snack.

Your postal carrier and local post office employees are probably the government employees with whom you have the greatest contact, and on whom you most rely on a daily basis!

Other Mail Handlers

The kindness you extend to your mail carrier can and should also be extended to others who process the mail in your place of business—the mail room personnel who are on the front line when it comes to handling any suspicious or dangerous packages and letters. Private mail and package carriers will also appreciate being thanked.

Don't ridicule those who take caution in opening or handling your mail. Share any safety tips you hear about how to detect parcels or letters that may have dangerous items in them.

If you detect any suspicious mail, leave the mail where you opened it or found it, wash your hands thoroughly with soap and warm water, and then call for emergency help.

Help the Less Fortunate

What the people want is very simple. They want an America as good as its promise.

—BARBARA JORDAN

TAKE A WALK TO YOUR PANTRY or food cabinet and open the door. Take out all the cans and containers of food that have been on the shelf for more than three months and place them on the nearest counter. Have you run out of countertop space yet?

Most of us forget that there are hungry people in our city until Thanksgiving and Christmas when news agencies highlight the work of local charities who strive to feed the hungry throughout the year. Likewise, we forget that there are people walking the streets without adequate clothing and shoes until a local shelter puts out a plea for coats and blankets.

Sadly, these needs exist every day. There are people within a few miles of you at this moment who are hungry and need the food you placed on your countertop.

Volunteer to Help

Consider volunteering as part of the kitchen or serving crew at a local shelter. Help collect coats and blankets for people who will spend most of the winter in shelters or on the streets. Participate in a Christmas toy drive to benefit families who can't afford to buy presents for their children.

Feeding and clothing those who are in need isn't difficult and it need not be time consuming. All it requires is an hour every three months or so. First, obtain several sturdy, stackable containers that you can carry alone when filled. Label each container with a category such as "kid's clothes," "women's," "canned goods," and so forth. You might also put the name, address, and phone number of the charitable organization to which you anticipate donating the items. Find a corner of a closet or garage where they can be stored. Then do the following:

★ Clean out one drawer, closet, or shelf at the same time each week and place unneeded items—new or clean, gently worn—in the appropriate container.

★ When all the containers destined for the same place are full, call the charity and arrange for a pickup or delivery at a time convenient for you. Some charities such as Good Will and the Salvation Army have convenient, manned drop-off posts.

★ Don't forget that all your donations are tax deductible.

Help Build a Habitat House

Homelessness comes in many varieties. There are many fully employed families who still cannot afford housing. Hoping to keep life as normal as possible for their children, some begin camping out in their cars and washing in public restrooms so their children can continue to attend their regular schools.

Still others find their dilapidated rental housing suddenly condemned. Unable to find other affordable housing, they stay with friends and relatives while they search for housing. But moving always brings new expenses, such as deposits and payment of first and last month's rent. Many could make modest house payments, but they could never afford the down payment and other expenses that go along with buying a modest home.

You can help someone realize the American dream in a concrete way by volunteering to help build a house with Habitat for Humanity. Habitat homes are built completely with donations of materials and labor. Even people who have never used a hammer or paintbrush can help construct a home for a struggling family. Once built, the family has new, clean, attractive housing (usually for the first time in their lives) with payments that are affordable. By working on a Habitat House, you not only provide shelter but also a huge dose of dignity.

Evaluating a Charitable Organization

How do you decide which organizations to support with your time, effort, and money? Most large, well-known national organizations are ethically managed and do an excellent job of delivering the services they promise to people in need. If you are distrustful, there are two rules of thumb to follow:

First, stick close to home. Give to organizations who will use what you donate to help those in your area.

Second, work *with* them. Don't just give money and cast-off goods. Volunteer your time and see how things are run within the organization. Talk to the people who use their services and find out what they think. Do you sense that the first concern of those who work for the charity is the well-being of the people they profess to serve? If so, put on your servant's hat and dig in. You're in the right place.

Remember that the possessions you own can disappear in a moment's time. But the good that you do by sharing what you have with others makes a lasting impression that will multiply as the recipients learn the blessings of giving.

59

17

Take Pride in American Productivity

60

Everything that is really great and inspiring is created by individuals who labor in freedom.

—ALBERT EINSTEIN

ONE OF THE FOREMOST WAYS of expressing patriotism is to buy American. When you purchase products made in America, you give a silent, economic vote in favor of America's ingenuity, productivity, and economic future.

Learn about American Inventors and Innovators

Millions of products, as well as millions of procedures, processes, and methods, have been created by American inventors. Millions more songs, musical scores, books, plays, screenplays, sculptures, paintings, dances, and theatrical presentations have been written, composed, or created by American artisans, authors, and musicians. Around the world, Americans have a strong reputation for bold, vibrant, creative expression and for the invention of both goods and services.

Set a goal for yourself to read at least one biography or autobiography a year about an American inventor or innovative artisan. Be inspired by their personal stories. You'll gain valuable insight into the relationship between freedom of speech and freedom to create. You'll also gain insight into how these two freedoms translate into economic bonanzas.

Overcoming the Criticisms

 61

Two main criticisms seem to be leveled at American products: They are expensive, and they are of lesser quality than foreign goods and services. In the majority of cases—and given that you get what you pay for—both of these criticisms tend to be false. Each of us, however, can do a great deal to overcome these criticisms as an act of our personal pride in our nation.

First, we can choose to purchase American products even in cases where the items may be a few cents more than foreign-manufactured items. Consider those extra few cents as the cost of stimulating the American economy and funding the future research and development necessary for innovation.

As part of choosing to buy American, you can also choose to invest in American companies. If Americans don't purchase stock in American corporations, buy real estate on American soil, or purchase American utility, municipal, and other government bonds, foreign investors will! One of the greatest unsung acts of personal patriotism you can do with regularity is to invest a portion of your income each month in the companies that produce the products you use. Your role as a shareholder gives you a strong voice in offering suggestions about how a company might improve its products.

Second, we can choose to do our best in everything, and especially to give our best effort in the workplace. If American products are inferior, we have only ourselves to blame. Commentator and television personality Charles Osgood once wrote a poetic essay we each are wise to take to heart:

There once was a pretty good student,
Who sat in a pretty good class
And was taught by a pretty good teacher,
Who always let pretty good pass.
He wasn't terrific at reading,
He wasn't a whiz-bang at math,
But for him, education was leading
Straight down a pretty good path.
He didn't find school too exciting,
But he wanted to do pretty well,
And he did have some trouble with writing,
And nobody had taught him to spell.
When doing arithmetic problems,
Pretty good was regarded as fine.
Five plus five didn't always add up to 10,
A pretty good answer was nine.
The pretty good class that he sat in
Was part of a pretty good school.
And the student was not an exception,
On the contrary, he was the rule.
The pretty good school that he went to
Was there in a pretty good town.
And nobody there seemed to notice
He could not tell a verb from a noun.
The pretty good student in fact was
Part of a pretty good mob.

TAKE PRIDE IN AMERICAN PRODUCTIVITY

And the first time he knew what he lacked was
When he looked for a pretty good job.
It was then, when he sought a position,
He discovered that life could be tough.
And he soon had a sneaky suspicion
Pretty good might not be good enough.
The pretty good town in our story
Was part of a pretty good state,
Which had pretty good aspirations,
And prayed for a pretty good fate.
There once was a pretty good nation,
Pretty proud of the greatness it had,
Which learned much too late,
If you want to be great,
Pretty good is, in fact, pretty bad.

Reference: "The Osgood File" © *1986, CBS Inc.*

Speak Your Patriotism

64

God grants liberty only to those who love it, and are always ready to guard and defend it.

—DANIEL WEBSTER

DEFENDING YOUR NATION may mean fighting on a battlefield, but it may also mean defending your nation against verbal attacks. Everyone can defend America against malicious criticism or destructive, disrespectful bashing.

America is not perfect. No nation on earth is perfect. The remarkable thing about America is that it protects your right to say or express exactly that!

Freedom of speech is one of the most dearly held rights of the citizens of the United States. Although it is not a right in every country in the world, it is a freedom that is desired in every part of the world. The First Amendment of the U.S. Constitution guarantees freedom of speech along with freedom of religion, press, and assembly.

Not an Unlimited Freedom

Freedom of speech is necessary in a democracy where people need to be informed in order to be good citizens. Freedom of speech, however, is not an absolute freedom. Our nation's laws restrict or prohibit many kinds of expression:

★ Libel and slander—written and verbal messages that are untrue, unjust, or regarded as damaging to a person's reputation

★ Speech that threatens national security

★ Obscenity

★ Speech that disrupts public order

★ Hate speech directed at racial or other groups

★ Sexual harassment

Even with restrictions, however, speech is freer in the United States than in most other nations.

Eight Positive Ways to Speak Your Patriotism

Since what we say can influence or affect many people, freedom of speech is a privilege that should inspire responsibility. Here are eight ways to speak your patriotism in a positive, responsible manner:

1. Choose your words wisely when speaking about America. Being a citizen of a nation is like being a member of a family—show respect for those you care about and who care about you. Wherever you go in the world, remember that you are a representative of your family and your nation.

2. Actively debate those who advocate anarchism or totalitarianism. Learn enough about other forms of political organization to expose their weaknesses. Develop your own arguments that demonstrate the value of democracy (for example, democracy results in the greatest good for the greatest

number of people; democracy protects the rights of minority citizens). Demonstrate the skills of a good debater: Have the facts; appeal to reason, not to emotion; acknowledge the good points that your opponent makes; don't make sweeping generalities that are not always true.

3. When defending your nation, it isn't necessary to gloss over or deny mistakes or bad choices made by government officials. Move quickly to the positive, however. Point out how those mistakes and bad judgments might be addressed and corrected. For example, you might acknowledge a weakness of our nation, such as a high crime rate, even as you point to ways in which various people and organizations are working to lower the crime rate.

4. Avoid the broad generalizations of extreme nationalism. An attitude such as "my country right or wrong" may mean that a person is willing to turn a blind eye and a deaf ear to areas that need change or improvement.

5. Say something good about your country's basic values and freedoms. Even if you disagree with a specific government policy, acknowledge that your government gives you the right to say so, and it will protect your right to disagree and dissent.

6. Be courteous and respectful to those who disagree with you and listen carefully to what they say. Their criticism may be constructive. Recognize, however, that a high percentage of criticism is intended to tear down traditional institutions or misconstrue facts. Know your facts so that you can counter misunderstandings. Especially know the documents on which your freedoms are based, such as the Declaration of Independence and the Constitution of the United States.

7. In discussions, avoid using labels or words that are inflammatory or antagonistic. Also avoid use of the words "al-

ways" and "never." Choose phrases such as "perhaps you might consider" instead of "you must agree." Keep your discussion objective.

8. Recognize that not all nations hold the same values as America: a high degree of independence, the right of minorities, and the right to pursue individual dreams and goals. You may need to decide to disagree agreeably.

If you are traveling in another nation, encourage patriotism as a virtue for every citizen. Each person can find something good about the nation in which he or she lives—that good may be the heritage, food, culture, people, or geography. Every nation has strengths. In speaking about the good values and virtues of America, recognize that other nations also have good qualities.

19

Get Involved in a Local Place of Worship

No people can be bound to acknowledge and adore the Invisible Hand which conducts the affairs of men more than those of the United States.

—GEORGE WASHINGTON

OUR NATION WAS ESTABLISHED by people who were seeking not only freedom from political tyranny, but also by people who were seeking religious freedom. A reliance upon and appeal to God was given reference in the Declaration of Independence, which boldly declares among its first words: "We hold these truths to be self-evident, that all men are created equal, that they are endowed by their Creator with certain unalienable Rights." The Founders of our nation went on to make this statement part of the first amendment to the Constitution:

Congress shall make no law respecting an establishment of religion, or prohibiting the free exercise thereof.

"In God We Trust" was adopted as the official national motto by the Founding Fathers, and that phrase was subsequently minted onto U.S. coins. Our nation adopted judicial and public office swearing-in oaths that call upon persons to declare that they will tell the whole truth and nothing but the truth, or render civil service using the phrase "so help me God."

69

An Ongoing Commitment to Religious Freedom

The references to God are not limited to the first decades of our nation, however. The phrase "under God" was added to the Pledge of Allegiance in 1953. A number of well-known patriotic statements made reference to God and to the freedom of religion in the 1940s.

Wendell Wilkie, an industrialist who challenged Franklin D. Roosevelt for the presidency in 1940, began his popular essay titled "Why I Believe in America" by writing, "I believe in America because in it we are free—free to choose our government, to speak our minds, to observe our different religions."

In 1946—after several tours ministering to the spiritual needs of American troops in Europe and Japan—Francis Cardinal Spellman wrote a similar piece entitled "An American Creed." It began with these words: "I believe in America: In her high destiny under God to stand before the people of the earth as a shining example of unselfish devotion to the ideals that have made us a great nation: the Christian ideal of liberty in harmonious unity, builded of respect for God's image in man and every man's right to life, liberty, and happiness."

Ensuring Religious Freedom

Many believe that the Bill of Rights calls for a total separation of church and state. That concept is not expressed by the Constitution but rather was a concept introduced by Thomas Jefferson in later writings. What the Bill of Rights does ensure is that the United States government will not impose a national or "state" religion upon the people. The Bill of Rights also ensures that the government will not prohibit the free exercise of religious practices and beliefs.

Although many of the Founding Fathers were Christians, not all were. One of the most popular writers at the time our nation was founded, Thomas Paine, wrote this in *The Age of Reason*: "I believe in one God, and no more; and I hope for happiness beyond this life. I believe in the equality of man; and I believe that religious duties consist in doing justice, loving mercy, and endeavoring to make our fellow-creatures happy. . . . I do not believe in the creed professed by the Jewish church, by the Roman church, by the Greek church, by the Turkish church, by the Protestant church, nor by any church that I know of. My own mind is my church." While Paine may have been a lonely congregation of one, his opinions underscored the belief of virtually all of the Founding Fathers: People of *all* religions should find freedom to exercise their religion in America.

The old adage "use it or lose it" may very well apply to this provision of freedom—if we fail to exercise our religious freedom, we are in danger of losing it. One of the prime ways to avoid either the imposition or elimination of religion is to become actively involved in a local place of worship.

Worship and Patriotism

The Reverend Ralph W. Sockman said, "Government laws are needed to give us civil rights, and God is needed to make us civil." This is the prevailing approach of the majority of religions—religion is linked strongly to civil behavior and to upholding a rule of order and law. Good faith and good citizenship are seen as walking hand in hand. Most hymnals in major denominations include patriotic songs; conversely, most political and civic meetings include some form of prayer or recognition of God. Prayers for our nation are routinely offered in many religious communities, many of whom have taken to heart this admonition from the New Testament, "I exhort first of all that supplications, prayers, intercessions, and giving of thanks be made for all men, for kings and all who are in authority, that we may lead a quiet and peaceable life in all godliness and reverence" (1 Timothy 2:1–2).

Church and state may remain organizationally independent in our nation, but prayer and a spirit of patriotism are common to both.

20 Participate in Local Government

The only thing necessary for the triumph of evil is for good men to do nothing.

—EDMUND BURKE

THE HIGH DRAMA AND HIGH STAKES of national politics and international events naturally command our attention. By contrast, matters of local governments seem mundane and routine. But it is at the local level that an individual can have a significant impact because, generally speaking, local government is more responsive to citizens' wishes and provides more opportunities for involvement than state or federal government. City and county governments and school districts are all considered local governments.

Local governments deal with issues that impact our lives most directly. For example, they decide commercial and residential zoning issues, and where to build streets and highways in a town. They determine local speed limits, set traffic lights, and provide police and fire protection. Local officials vote on public utility matters, oversee the local courts, assess property values, collect property taxes, and run the public school system.

Run for Office or Volunteer

What is the most effective way to participate in city government? The foremost way, of course, is to be elected mayor, city councilor, school board member, or county commissioner! Holding office, however, is not the only way you can impact your city or county.

Private citizens are needed to serve on city boards and commissions. These can be elected, appointed, or volunteer positions. Let your representative know you are interested in serving your community in this way and ask him or her to help you find a place to serve.

Participate in Local Politics

Attend the meetings of your local governments—city council, county commissioners, town hall, and school board. These meetings welcome public participation. By attending local meetings, you can be an eyewitness to government in action and learn how it functions. When citizens are given opportunity to speak their opinion, do so. Do your homework in advance—research information on all sides of the issue.

Circulate petitions on issues about which you feel strongly. If you don't think your one voice is getting enough attention, then gather signatures from other voters who think and believe the way you do.

Hold your legislators accountable to vote in the way they promised they would when they campaigned for election. If they back down from their campaign platform, call it to their attention and to the attention of the city through letters to the editor of the local newspaper.

If you aren't ready to run for office but want to get more involved in your city, try volunteering for city programs and services. Being a volunteer is often the first step toward an elected or appointed position. It lets people know you are serious about the well-being of your school district or city.

Visit Your State Legislature

74

One of the first ways to be informed about state government is to spend a day in the state legislature. You can watch debates and see the legislative process. If you desire to meet your representative, be sure to call, write, or email your request several weeks in advance of your visit.

Even if you cannot attend a session of the state legislature, you can follow a bill through the legislative process from the time it is introduced as a bill on the floor of the state congress, through the committees that make recommendations, to the actual House or Senate vote. The more you learn about how a bill becomes a law, the more effective and influential you will be in getting legislation *you* desire considered or enacted!

21 Seek Peace

'Tis not in numbers but in unity that our great strength lies.

—THOMAS PAINE

75

"LET THERE BE PEACE ON EARTH and let it begin in me" are the words of a song familiar to many Americans. Written by Sy Miller and Bill Jackson in 1955, this song signals the key to peace throughout the world: Peace is the responsibility of every person.

When people think of peace, they think of global peace among nations of the world. But conflict is a part of the everyday life of most individuals. There is conflict in the workplace, the classroom, the home, the place of worship, the courtroom, the marketplace—in fact, there is conflict wherever there are people. So, making peace is not about eliminating conflict. It is about agreeing to disagree and living peaceably with our differences. In a world of conflict and disagreement, getting along with people is just as important a skill as learning to use a computer.

Peace Begins at Home

Probably the most difficult conflicts are those in the family because there is nowhere to escape. The incidence of domestic violence and divorce so prevalent in modern culture is a strong indicator of our need to learn how to resolve differences first and foremost *at home*.

An intriguing statistic emerged following the September 11, 2001, terrorist attacks on the World Trade Center. Harris County in Texas reported that the number of dismissals in divorce cases skyrocketed three times more than the usual rate in the days following the attacks. Couples reconsidered their priorities in light of the attacks and decided to try to reconcile their differences to keep their families together. Don't give up on difficult relationships without going the second, third, and fourth mile!

Apologies and Forgiveness

Probably the first and foremost way to make peace is to learn to say, "I'm sorry" and "Forgive me." Everybody makes mistakes and everybody needs to be forgiven at some time or another. To apologize and sincerely ask for forgiveness is a way to bring peace. No one is perfect. The familiar saying is still true: To err is human, to forgive is divine.

It may be easy to say words of forgiveness, but the challenge is to live out the forgiveness process—to change your ways and live as though you are forgiven, and to truly work for the good and benefit of the person who has been wronged or who wronged you. Keep taking small steps—do an act of kindness for the other person, write a note, or make a call to let the person know you are sincere in wanting a new beginning and a fresh start.

The Bible gives wise advice: "Don't let the sun go down on your anger." Wrongdoings add up to create bitterness and deep resentment. Deal with upsets and affronts on a consistent, regular basis and you will find mountains have been turned into molehills!

Try to understand the other person's point of view as you seek to resolve misunderstandings. Take time to really listen to the offender's grievances and see the argument from his or her point of view. Then, together explore ways to mutually agree or compromise.

Take the Initiative

Take the initiative to work out differences or call a truce to bring an end to a longstanding dispute—don't wait for the other person to come to you. Taking that first step is risky because you face possible rejection. It very well might be that the other person is waiting for you! Often priorities change and attitudes soften in the wake of a disagreement or time of estrangement. Now may be the right time to initiate a peace-making offer!

Mediation

Schools, workplaces, and courts are beginning to use the services of professional mediators. You may want to enlist the help of a neutral, mutually respected, trustworthy mediator—either a friend who knows both sides of the dispute or a professional counselor.

Far too much energy and time is spent in getting even or bearing a grudge—whether it is at the family, local, national, or international level. Take the first step today to be a peacemaker.

22 Say "No" to Hate Groups

I realize that patriotism is not enough. I must have no hatred or bitterness towards anyone.

—EDITH CAVELL

"TEARING DOWN IS EASY," a demolition expert once noted. "It's building that's tough." What is true for concrete and steel is even more true for human relations and for the cherished institutions associated with freedom.It takes only a few people and a few seconds to destroy a life, a building, or a tradition.

Start with Your Own Heart

All acts of patriotism and all acts of destruction begin in the same place—in the heart and mind of a single individual. Most acts of destruction are rooted in bigotry, prejudice, or hatred for a particular person, group of people, institution, or cultural practice. Take a moment to stare into your own heart and ask, "Who do I hate? What are my prejudices? Who do I blame for what I perceive as being a grievous negative circumstance? Is there some person or a group that automatically seems to evoke anger in me?"

Then ask, "Why do I hold this hatred and anger?" The honest person is likely to admit at least some bias or prejudice, and the reflective person is also likely to admit that he came to this bias or prejudice because he was *taught* to hate.

Choose to rethink your hatred. Get more information about the people or group you *think* you are justified in hating. Seek to converse with a person against whom you hold prejudice. Together explore what might be common ground between you. You may be surprised that the person against whom you are prejudiced is equally prejudiced against you—also as a result of inadequate information or experience!

Drop Your Affiliation

If you are a part of any group that takes a militant stand against another person or group of people solely on the basis of race, culture, ethnicity, religion, age, or sex, drop your affiliation. If you are part of a group that excludes others from membership solely on the basis of race, culture, ethnicity, religion, age, or sex, drop your membership.

Say "No" to Destruction and Denigration

Part of upholding the dignity of all Americans is to say "no" to anything that destroys or belittles the institutions and practices associated with our basic freedoms.

★ Teach your children to say "no" to bullying—to refuse to bully others and to refuse to be bullied. The majority of people who bully others continue to do so because their behavior is never confronted or challenged.

★ Refuse to limit your associations to a clique. Encourage

your children to broaden their horizons and have friends of many ethnicities, cultures, and races.

★ Do not allow your children to speak ill of a person's race, age, sex, ethnicity, culture, or religion. Watch your own speech. Cut out all racial slurs and refuse to listen to or repeat racial or ethnic jokes. Let others know that you are offended by such remarks.

★ If a hate group seeks to recruit you, refuse the invitation. You don't need to justify your position. Just say "no."

★ If a hate group seeks to rally in your neighborhood or community, speak out against the meeting. Write a letter to the editor of your local newspaper, call a local talk show, or show up with a placard of your own that stands in opposition to their meeting. Encourage others to join you in protesting the meeting, convention, or rally of those who ultimately seek to destroy a part of your community by destroying the morale or lives of the citizens in your community. Make hate unwelcome in your city.

★ Openly discuss certain hate groups with your teenagers. Explain their purposes and intentions. Let your child know that you do not support their agendas.

One of the most famous speeches in our nation's history is George Washington's Farewell Address. This speech was once memorized by most school children in America. Washington made these statements in his speech: "Be Americans. . . . Let there be no sectionalism, no North, South, East or West; you are all dependent one on another, and should be one in union. . . . Beware of the baneful effects of party spirit and of the ruin to which its extremes must lead. . . . Have neither passionate hatreds nor passionate attachments to any."

It is American to peacefully disagree.

It is un-American to hate.

23 Revisit the Declaration of Independence

The Declaration of Independence was a vital piece of practical business, not a piece of rhetoric.

—WOODROW WILSON

T HE DECLARATION OF INDEPENDENCE—adopted by the Continental Congress on July 4, 1776— proclaimed to the world the independence of the thirteen colonies of Great Britain in America, and marked the birth of a new nation. Most Americans know those facts as a result of having read or studied the Declaration in school. What many Americans do not know is this:

★ The Declaration did not initiate the Revolutionary War. When the Declaration was signed, actual warfare to drive out the forces of the mother country had already begun. The battles of Lexington and Concord and Bunker Hill had been fought. Forts Ticonderoga and Crown Point had already been taken from the British. George Washington had been appointed commander-in-chief of our army. A petition *requesting* freedom had been sent to King George III. New Hampshire and South Carolina had already set up independent colonial governments.

★ Early in 1776, several delegates to the Continental Congress were instructed by their constituents to vote for a formal statement of independence. On May 15, 1776, Congress adopted a resolution advising all colonies to follow the example of Massachusetts, New Hampshire, and South Carolina in setting up colonial governments. Then on June 7, Richard Henry Lee of Virginia moved:

"That these United Colonies are, and of right ought to be, free and independent States; that they are absolved from all allegiance to the British Crown, and that all political connection between them and the State of Great Britain is, and ought to be, totally dissolved;

"That it is expedient forthwith to take the most effectual measures for forming foreign alliances;

"That a plan of confederation be prepared and transmitted to the respective colonies for their consideration and approbation."

His motion was seconded by John Adams of Massachusetts, debated on June 8 and 10, and then further action was postponed until all the colonies could act. On June 10 a committee was appointed to "prepare a Declaration."

★ The Declaration was written primarily by Thomas Jefferson, who served as chairman of the Committee on Declaration. He was assisted by John Adams, Benjamin Franklin, Roger Sherman, and Robert R. Livingston. The document was written over a period of eighteen days and the final report was distributed to the Continental Congress delegates on June 28.

★ The adoption of the Declaration was the climax of four intense days of debate that began on July 1. The Congress formed itself into a "committee of the whole" and sat behind closed doors while the debate took place. John Adams delivered a speech in favor of the resolution and his speech was so effective that Thomas Jefferson later called Adams the "Colossus of that debate." Lee's motion was formally adopted on July 2—it is this motion that legally set into place the framework for establishing our nation. On July 3 the Declaration itself was debated. The Declaration was passed and published on July 4.

★ The Declaration that was passed was shorter than the Declaration initially drafted by Jefferson and his committee. During the debate on the Declaration, several amendments were proposed and adopted, which resulted in several segments of the document being deleted.

★ Fifty-six delegates signed the Declaration. Delegates from twelve colonies signed the document on July 4. New York added its vote on July 9.

The Declaration Document

Although the Declaration of Independence is the cornerstone of our nation as a political entity, many Americans have never read the Declaration in its entirety. Those who do read it are generally surprised to see that much of the Declaration is devoted to listing perceived wrongs committed by the King of England. The Declaration states: "The history of the present King of Great Britain is a history of repeated injuries and usurpations." The Declaration concludes, "A Prince whose character is thus marked by every act which may define a Tyrant, is unfit to be the ruler of a free people."

While the preamble to the Declaration is perhaps best known, the concluding paragraph of the Declaration is what "declares" our sovereignty as a nation: "We, therefore, the Representatives of the united States of America, in General Congress, Assembled, appealing to the Supreme Judge of the world for the rectitude of our intentions, do, in the Name, and by Authority of the good People of these Colonies, solemnly publish and declare, That these United Colonies are, and of Right ought to be Free and Independent States; that they are Absolved from all Allegiance to the British Crown, and that all political connection between them and the State of Great Britain, is and ought to be totally dissolved; and that as Free and Independent States, they have full Power to levy War, conclude Peace, contract Alliances, establish Commerce, and to do all other Acts and Things which Independent States may of right do. And for the support of this Declaration, with a firm reliance on the protection of divine Providence, we mutually pledge to each other our Lives, our Fortunes and our sacred Honor."

84

The original Declaration of Independence document has been in the care of the Library of Congress since 1921. It is sealed in a steel case to protect it from light and air and thus preserved as one of the nation's priceless relics.

Note: The Declaration of Independence can be found in appendix A.

24 Revisit the Constitution and Bill of Rights

85

Let us then stand by the Constitution as it is,
and by our country as it is, united, and entire;
let it be a truth engraven on our hearts.

—DANIEL WEBSTER

The Constitution was actually developed because serious defects became apparent in the "Articles of Confederation," which was the initial governing document adopted by the Congress in 1781. Initially the colonies had been loosely organized as a "league of sovereign states." This organizational pattern did not allow for the regulation of foreign and interstate commerce, so a special convention was called with the express purpose of revising the Articles of Confederation.

The convention met under the presidency of George Washington. Sixty-five members were appointed to the convention by the states but only fifty-five delegates were able to attend. The convention worked four months in drafting the Constitution, with several major conflicts and subsequent debates emerging over issues related to the presidency, division of power between large and small states, slavery, and the means of electing the president.

The Constitution Document

Those who take the time to read the Constitution are often surprised at what is and isn't covered in the articles and amendments. Many are surprised at the Old English spellings of the words "chuse" and "behaviour." The Constitution has seven articles. The general content of these articles is as follows:

★ Article I—Organization of legislative departments and the powers of Congress

★ Article II—The executive department, powers and duties of the president, and manner of election

★ Article III—The organization of the judicial department, and the extent of its powers

★ Article IV—Powers granted to the states

★ Article V—Method of amendment

★ Article VI—Validity of contracts prior to adoption of the Constitution, the supremacy of the Constitution, and oath or affirmation required of officials

★ Article VI—Ratification necessary to put the Constitution into effect

Adoption and Amendments

Of the fifty-five members present at the convention, only thirty-nine signed the final document that was drafted. Sixteen delegates either refused to sign or left the convention before the document was completed. Ratification was required by only nine states for the Constitution to become the supreme law of the land. Eventually, however, all thirteen states ratified it, although the vote in many states was far from unanimous. Rhode Island, for example, supported the Constitution by a vote of thirty-four to thirty-two.

Ratification of the Constitution took more than two years—from Delaware's unanimous vote on December 7, 1787, to Rhode Island's reluctant vote on May 29, 1790.

Through the centuries, the Constitution has been praised around the world for its innovation in providing a "balance of power" among legislative, executive, and judicial branches of government. Thomas Jefferson said of the document, "The Constitution of the United States is the result of the collected wisdom of our country."

The Bill of Rights

The main opposition to the Constitution's ratification was a conviction that the rights of the people had not been sufficiently safeguarded. It was only on the definite understanding that the first Congress would correct the omission by proposing amendments that several states voted to ratify the document. The first ten amendments—called the Bill of Rights—were proposed in 1789 and adopted in 1791.

Note: The Constitution and the Bill of Rights can be found in appendixes B and C.

Say "Please" and "Thank You"

It is sweet to serve one's country by deeds, and it is not absurd to serve her by words.

—SALLUST

AS A YOUNG MAN in the early eighteenth century, George Washington wrote out by hand a list of 110 rules for civil behavior. He kept this list with him from Valley Forge to Yorktown and throughout the terms of his presidency. Showing respect to and getting along with people were essential to character, and success without character, Washington held, was worthless. Among the rules were a number that called for being careful of what you say to show respect for the other person.

Rule #49 in George Washington's "Rules of Civility" states: "Use no reproachful language against any one, neither curse nor revile." Rule #65 says: "Speak not injurious words neither in jest nor earnest; scoff at none although they give occasion."

Those same rules would serve us well in our modern society that has been characterized as increasingly rude and uncivil. We are all affected by the frequent rude behavior that has infiltrated society—from driving practices to shock talk shows to flaunting the violation of manners of common politeness and courtesy.

When we encounter rude or unkind behavior, it is easy to respond in the same way—to fail to return phone calls or behave impatiently while waiting in the checkout line. The key to civil and gracious behavior is not to respond as you are being treated, but to respond and behave as you would like to be treated.

Common Courtesies

Use this list of common courtesies as a starting point to compiling your own list.

1. When you receive a formal dinner or wedding invitation that requests a reply, do so within the timeframe specified and then follow through on what you said you would do.

2. Be on time. If you are running late for an appointment, call ahead to let the person know when you can be expected. Planning ahead will help you to be prompt and not keep others waiting. Respect their time as well as your own.

3. Give others the benefit of the doubt if you are hurt by what someone else has said. Assume that the other's comments were not intended to be hurtful.

4. When you are conversing with another person, listen closely to what he or she is saying and ignore distractions in order to give that person your full attention.

5. Be the one to extend common courtesies when driving. Road rage is a frequent phenomena and can cause accidents. If someone is driving recklessly or dangerously close, get out of the way of that driver. If necessary turn onto another street to let him or her get by.

6. Turn off your cell phone when it would be inappropriate to be interrupted or be a distraction to others. When you do need to take or make an important call, leave the room so your conversation doesn't interrupt others.

7. Keep confidences. When someone has trusted you enough to confide in you, respect that person by keeping the information to yourself. Live up to the trust that person has placed in you.

8. Welcome the stranger in your midst. When a new employee joins the workforce or a new neighbor moves to your block, extend a warm and personal welcome.

9. Don't disturb others by talking in a movie theater, concert, or worship service. Use headphones if you are listening to music, and turn down the noise from a beeper, cell phone, or laptop computer.

10. Actions speak louder than words. Be a model of respect and courtesy to others and you will be a positive influence to increase the civility needed in our culture.

Putting the "Civil" into Civilization

Like George Washington, make your own 110 rules for civil behavior. Expand the list above by adding your ideas based on how you would like to be treated. And then practice them! You will be surprised at how much you can reduce stresses in your life and maybe even make a positive difference in another person's day by showing some simple kindness.

By observing some basic guidelines of courteous and gracious behavior, you can help build a society in which people are treated with respect and courtesy—and when people are treated that way, they tend to become respectful and courteous. A free society that exists for the common good of all people requires a show of mutual respect and courtesy.

26 Play a History Hunt Game

It is refreshing to turn to the early incidents of our history, and learn wisdom from the acts of the great men who have gone to their account.

—John McLean

91

ISTORY MAY SOUND BORING to some children because it's a school subject. Children who love mysteries will soon realize that the history of our country is full of intrigue and surprises worthy of their mystery-solving talents once the History Hunt gets underway.

This is a learning experience that can be fun for everyone in your family. If you have children over the age of nine or ten years, you can add the element of "why?" into the game and watch their critical reasoning skills blossom. But that's just a bonus. Ultimately, children and adults alike will gain a much greater appreciation for the people who founded our nation and made our freedom possible.

Here are some basic ideas to get you started.

★ Introduce the idea to your kids as a "game." Have a family meeting to pick out a name (such as, The Jones History Detective Agency).

★ Agree on a regular meeting time to "discuss the case"—allow about fifteen to twenty minutes one or two days a week.

★ Choose a character from our nation's history (or the history of your state) to investigate.

★ Try to have a specific question that everyone is working toward answering. For example, "Did he die of natural causes or could his enemies have done him in?"

★ Begin the case by getting a brief biography of the chosen person to share at the first meeting. Brief biographies of many of our nation's founders are online at: www.colonialhall.com/biodoi.asp.

★ Assign specific "stakeouts" to each child *and* each parent. For instance, daughter will find out who the founder's children were and what became of them. Son and dad could find out what business he was in before he began serving our nation and who his enemies might have been. Mom might find out some things about the spouse and the spouse's family or other family members.

★ Encourage everyone to bring any bits of information to the meeting. Ask children to tell what they have found.

★ Be sure to schedule sleuthing trips to the library (even if you have a computer and other materials at your home). Exposing children to new sources of information is an important part of maintaining interest in the game.

★ If you live in an area where you can visit historic places associated with the person under investigation, be sure to plan a trip.

★ Use a chalkboard or large sheet of paper to chart your findings. Draw a family tree for the person in one color and use different colors to show other characters.

★ Use pictures of the character and his family and associates to help put a face on the characters.

★ Use maps to help identify distances people had to travel to participate in government and talk about how travel was different for the character.

★ When everyone thinks all the evidence is gathered, vote on your "solution" to the mystery question you have imposed.

★ Record your "detective agency's" findings in a notebook or journal.

★ Use a large manila folder to store the pictures, maps, charts, etc., from the group's work.

Each parent who begins the game can add and remove elements from the suggested list of activities above—just remember to keep it a game. If your children begin to tell you they don't need extra "homework," you'll know it's not a game any more. Simplify the game or offer a small reward for digging up a particular piece of information.

If you don't have a home computer, you may want to plan to spend a little more time in the public library where access to information on the web is available for free and librarians are present to help children with their search skills.

Finally, consider treating the whole family to a trip to Washington, D.C., Philadelphia, Gettysburg, or other historic areas when you've completed several cases. The visit will be much richer for each member of the family if you have played the History Hunt.

27 Visit Our Nation's Memorials and Parks

A free, virtuous, and enlightened people must know full well the great principles and causes upon which their happiness depends.

—JAMES MONROE

OUR NATION IS BLESSED with a wealth of natural beauty, historic sites, and outstanding recreational areas under the oversight of the National Park Service. The government has set aside more than 350 such areas, protecting them from development to make them available and accessible for visitors. These sites include national parks, monuments, historic sites, memorials, cemeteries, seashores, lakeshores, and battlefields. The areas set aside have been selected for their beautiful natural features, historic value, or recreational features.

Our National Parks

The national parks are particularly popular destinations for family vacations since they offer recreation, adventure, and hands-on education in the natural sciences. The key to making your trip to a national park memorable is to plan ahead. The National Park Service provides valuable information through its web site at www.nps.gov.

★ *What to Do.* What is your favorite recreation—hiking, mountain climbing, sea kayaking, cross-country skiing, backpacking, swimming, boating, fishing, river rafting, bird watching, snowmobiling, horseback riding? All these activities and more are available in our national parks. Some of the national parks even offer education and camp institutes for families to learn the natural history and ecology of the park.

★ *Where to Go.* Where you go depends on what you want to do. There are over fifty national parks to choose from, at least one in each major section of the country. Acadia National Park in Maine and Port Reyes Park in California are great places to go for whale watching. Cross-country skiing is available in Bryce Canyon in Utah, Sequoia National Park in California, and Yellowstone in Wyoming. Hiking and walking trails are options in nearly all the parks.

★ *When to Go.* The most popular vacation time is when schools are out in the summer and during spring and winter breaks. If you are traveling at peak season, be sure to plan ahead to get reservations. To beat the crowds, however, the best time is off-season during the weeks and months closest to the best-weather months.

★ *How to Get There.* A car is a necessity at nearly every park. So, if you plan to fly to your destination, also plan to reserve a rental car for your travel to and around the park.

★ *Where to Stay*. National parks offer both hotel accommodations and campground spaces. Check ahead to find out if the park you are visiting offers campsite reservations. Some operate on a first come, first served basis.

★ *Who Will Be Traveling*. Parks are fabulous for memory-making family vacations, so if you will be traveling with children, plan ahead to take advantage of age-appropriate activities. Younger children do better exploring national seashores and coastal parks. Save strenuous hiking in the more challenging wilderness parks for older children and teens.

96

National Monuments and Memorials

In addition to the national parks, the National Park System has twenty different types of protected areas. These include national monuments, memorials, and historic sites. There are currently twenty-eight national memorials that commemorate historic people or episodes in our nation's history, but they are not necessarily on the actual historic site. Some of the more famous memorials are the Thomas Jefferson Memorial, Lincoln Memorial, and Washington Monument all in Washington, D.C., and the Mt. Rushmore National Memorial in Rapid City, South Dakota. The Korean War Veterans and Vietnam Veterans Memorials in Washington, D.C., and the USS Arizona Memorial in Pearl Harbor commemorate those who died in battles.

The Oklahoma City National Memorial stands in memory of those who died in the 1995 bombing of the Alfred P. Murrah Federal Building in Oklahoma City. The Wright Brothers National Memorial in Kill Devil Hills, North Carolina, pays tribute to the pioneering work of Wilbur and Orville Wright in the invention of the airplane. The Johnstown Flood National Memorial in Pennsylvania stands to remember the 1889 flood in which more than 2,200 died. This was also the site of the first Red Cross disaster relief effort led by Clara Barton.

Historic Sites

Historic sites are another category of places under governance by the National Park Service. Visiting these sites where the events of history took place brings the people and places of your American heritage to life. The most famous historical area is probably the White House in Washington, D.C.

Note: For a list of memorials, parks, and other patriotic sites *to visit go online to http://www.cr.nps.gov/nhl/travel.htm or www.nr.nps.gov.*

28 Learn about Your Community "Memorials"

Never doubt that a small group of thoughtful, committed citizens can change the world. Indeed it is the only thing that ever has.

—MARGARET MEAD

DO YOU KNOW THE STORIES of your local heroes? Do you know the history of the people who have made your city a great place to live? Do you know who founded your community and when? Is there a place in your city where the services and sacrifices of its veterans are remembered? Do they have any family or friends still living in your city?

Are there any small-town legends in your town's history—people who made a name for themselves and are remembered (perhaps even inaccurately as local folklore) for their colorful histories? Does your city have a claim to fame because one of its citizens left home and succeeded in a big way? There may be local tales to uncover about that person from people who knew them when. Don't ignore the ordinary people—those people described as the "salt of the earth" and "pillars of the community"—the solid citizens who contributed to the life of your town.

Where do you uncover the stories of the people who made your city a great place to live? If your city is large enough, you will no doubt find published histories that have been written in detail about the movers and shakers whose names are now on streets and parks and buildings. Even so, by digging into local libraries and newspaper archives you may uncover a new human-interest angle to that story that has been forgotten or lost in the archives.

A Published History for Your Community

If your town does not have a published history, you can start compiling your own. The place to begin is your public library, local newspaper, the internet, and the greatest resource— your town's senior citizens. Search the archives for names of the people who are part of your community heritage. You may find that there are living descendants who can tell you the stories they heard passed down about their "famous" relatives and what made them great.

Everybody has a story to tell. Ask around at a local senior citizen center to locate someone who may have information about your town fathers and mothers. They would be delighted to share their stories. Take along a tape recorder to record a first-person account. You may have the beginnings of an oral history of your city. Don't overlook your parents or grandparents who may have known local celebrities.

A Town Museum

Your city may have a local history association, but if not, you can start one. Ask your local librarian if the library might allocate an area for archives of your town's history. Your town may have an old schoolhouse or empty downtown building that could be renovated to house an exhibit of pictures and artifacts about your city's history. Gather a group of retired people to recall and help put the history together.

Time Capsules

Enlist teachers to involve their classes in collecting items for a time capsule to provide history to future generations. Carefully select artifacts that represent all facets of your city. A Memorial Day celebration or the anniversary of the founding of your town would be a great time to launch such an undertaking.

 100

Honor Senior Citizens

Honor the senior citizens of your organization, corporation, place of worship, or community with a luncheon or banquet. Let them know they are appreciated for the contributions they made to your community. Record the event on video for future generations and ask attendees to tell their favorite stories.

International Ties

The investigation into your community's history will most likely take you back to the Old World roots of your town's founders and early settlers. Finding those connections would be a great opportunity to establish a sister city relationship with a town or city in another country that was once home to your ancestors. Your local school may want to sponsor an exchange student from that country to live and study in your community.

You and the citizens of your community will be enriched by the stories of its founders and heroes. History is not just dust but a memory of heroes, both ordinary and extraordinary, who made your town a great place to live.

29 Take Care of Needy Children

If a man is fortunate he will, before he dies, gather up as much as he can of his civilized heritage and transmit it to his children.

—WILL DURANT

I T IS SAID THAT THE MORALITY of a nation is measured by how it treats its most vulnerable citizens. If so, then how Americans treat children, and especially needy children, is of great significance.

Providing for a family is a big responsibility. When a crisis strikes a family—for instance, the death of the breadwinner or a major disability or illness—it can become impossible to provide for the family's needs no matter how much the family wants to remain self-sufficient.

Fortunately, there are many public and private agencies that have as their purpose the protection of children and the care for their needs. While an agency can look after the physical and material needs of children, there is no question that caring individuals have great impact on a child's life.

One to One

Developing a one-on-one relationship with a needy child is one way to give that child a great gift—your undivided attention! Children often withdraw or behave badly because of stresses or problems in their homes that they don't know how to express. But children thrive when they know someone cares about them, when they have someone in their lives on whom they can depend and from whom they receive extra encouragement. Contact your local school district, house of worship, Big Sister or Big Brother program, or Boy Scouts or Girl Scouts to find out how you can get involved in a child's life.

Consistently and Reliably

When participating in such a program be consistent and reliable. Needy children often lack a stable home life—one of the parents may be absent, a parent may have to work two or more jobs to make ends meet, or the child may be living with a stepparent who is unable to give the child unconditional love. These children need adults they can count on to "be there" for them when *they* have needs, which is not necessarily when adults have inclination! One-on-one relationships take an abundance of time and flexibility.

Work through Agencies

Consider making a contribution to the Angel Tree program that provides Christmas presents for children of prisoners. Or lead or contribute to a drive to provide back-to-school school supplies. Give a scholarship to allow a child to go to summer camp with the YMCA or YWCA, or with the Scouts program. Donate your children's good used clothing to the Salvation Army or Goodwill.

A Wide Variety of Approaches

Be supportive of the child's parents to help them provide a stable home life. You can organize an after-school program for latchkey children to provide them a safe place to be before their parents return home from work. Call your local school district to ask if such a program exists where you can volunteer or to find out about starting such a service.

Often retired people enjoy being adopted grandparents to children who do not have a lot of parental support. Others get involved with organizations that help families get back together after a spouse leaves jail. These families face enormous challenges and need community support to stabilize their family life.

Set up a neighborhood watch to involve everyone in caring for children. People who prey on children are less likely to circulate through a neighborhood where neighbors are looking out for each other. Looking out for one another is a great way to build spirit and get to know your neighbors.

Reporting Abuse

The law requires that child abuse be reported to authorities. If you have reason to suspect that a child is living in an abusive home situation or is being neglected, report it to authorities.

There is no one telltale sign that a child is being abused. Physical injuries or bruises may indicate abuse. Other signs are less obvious. A child may have nightmares or trouble sleeping. Their school performance may decline suddenly, or the child may manifest behavior problems such as bullying, intense rage, or acting out in the classroom. They may have difficulty in forming friendships or being able to trust others.

They may also avoid going home after school or be fearful of certain adults. If you observe these signs, start asking questions. Don't accuse . . . but do ask.

Those who abuse children may show signs as well. For example, parents who abuse their children may avoid other parents in the neighborhood, may not participate in school activities, and may be uncomfortable talking about their children's injuries or behavioral problems.

If you suspect that a child is being abused, you have a legal responsibility to contact your local child protective services agency, police, hospital, or emergency hotline. If necessary, you may remain anonymous. The child's safety is the immediate issue: You could save his life.

Foster Parenting

You may want to consider becoming a foster parent to a child who is temporarily without a permanent home. The process of certification as a foster parent involves a formal interview, training classes, references, and a home inspection, but if you are willing to make this commitment, you are likely to find that you can have a great impact on a child by providing a secure and loving home.

Children are our greatest national resource. Choose to help a child who doesn't have all the advantages *every* child deserves.

30   Learn from the Elderly

The care of human life and happiness, and not their destruction, is the first and only legitimate object of good government.

—THOMAS JEFFERSON

105

I T'S A SIMPLE MATHEMATICAL FACT: Our senior citizens know the most about what it means to be an American. Now is the time to learn from them!

Approaching the Elderly

Being with elder adults can be a delightful experience. Many people, however, who have not had much exposure to frail, elderly people are hesitant and even a little afraid to interact with them. A visit to a long-term care facility can be daunting. Sometimes, the sight of disabled, dependent, and older individuals in a nursing home is disturbing.

Try to look beyond physical appearances. Think of each of these residents as interesting individuals who have experienced much in life. Each person has a unique personality that is not dependent upon physical appearance. You may be bothered by those who appear to be confused or disoriented. If you gently hold their hands and look into their eyes, you can comfort them.

Children are actually much more accepting of large groups of elder adults. The best way to prepare young children for a visit to a nursing home is to tell them everything you can about it. Patiently answer their questions. For example, tell them there will be people with wheelchairs and walkers, and some will be in bed. Say something like this: "Instead of living by herself now, grandmother lives with other people who can help take care of her." Explain that it may even smell different, like a hospital. Help children feel free to ask questions about the nursing home by always answering them truthfully.

Making the Most of Your Elder Visits

Here are some suggestions to make your time spent with older folks deeply rewarding for you both:

★ Try to think of the older person as being someone nearer your own age; they probably do.

★ Bring small, inexpensive gifts (like a bag of peppermints, a flower, or a homemade goodie) when you visit.

★ Speak clearly and distinctly, and avoid using too much slang.

★ Don't assume that just because they are old they have a problem hearing, seeing, or thinking. Do not speak louder to an elderly person unless you are asked to do so.

★ Be yourself.

★ Always arrange visits in advance. Remember that an older person may feel more energetic or social at certain times of the day.

★ Tell the nursing home, caregiver, or the elderly person if you will be bringing a child, pet, or another person with you.

★ Give some advanced thought to what you will do when you get there. Perhaps you can take a walk outside or visit another part of the nursing home.

★ Spend time reminiscing.

★ Ask the individual his or her opinion or to help you make some decisions about something in your life. Remember, this is a person who has lived a long time and whose wisdom is valuable.

★ Take the person out to lunch (or an early dinner) at a favorite restaurant or cafeteria.

★ Take the person to doctor's appointments or the grocery store or other shopping.

★ Read a story together or write letters. Concentrate on the quality of your visit.

★ Remember that most elderly adults do not enjoy visitors, calls, or activities after 7:30 or 8 P.M.

★ Do not promise to visit and then fail to show up. If you cannot keep an appointment, call in advance and immediately suggest a substitute time.

Becoming More Active with the Elderly

Here are some suggestions for becoming more active with the senior population:

★ Call your state nursing home ombudsman to find out how to volunteer in your area. You can locate your state's ombudsman at www.nursinghomeaction.org/static_pages/ombudsmen.cfm.

★ Visit your local senior citizen's center to find out what seniors programs need volunteers.

★ Be a mealtime companion for a nursing home resident. Residents who must eat alone often lose interest in meals and become malnourished or dehydrated—a life-threatening condition for frail seniors.

★ Lead a senior adults exercise class at your place of worship or local senior citizen's center.

★ Interview a senior adult about his or her life; ask lots of questions and ask to see their photographs.

★ If you enjoy writing, consider using your interview to write a story about his or her life and make copies for grandchildren or other relatives and friends.

31 Give to Charitable Organizations

*I have been seeing a lot of Americans lately,
and they all seem to have that kind of fervour
which means aiding and not hindering life.*

— ROBERT HUGH BENSON

TAX-EXEMPT ORGANIZATIONS are the fastest growing sector in the U.S. economy. About thirty thousand new charities are created each year. There are now 1.4 million nonprofit organizations, and the competition for funds is intense.

As charities face inflation, government budget cuts, and an increasing public demand for services, they are asking for more donations. More and more charities use high-tech fund-raising techniques. Mailboxes overflow with fund-raising appeals. Phone calls pour in from high-pressure solicitors. All this can leave us confused about which charities are most deserving of contributions.

Most charities are honest and accountable to their donors. Unfortunately, a few are not. Here are suggestions to help you give more effectively.

Take Control of Your Giving

Make a giving plan and budget each year. Decide what you can afford to give and the types of causes that you wish to support. Having a budget ensures that you will not forget to give and reminds you to set money aside for disaster relief or other immediate needs. Giving to charity is a social investment. Don't shortchange your investment in your community, whether it is your neighborhood, the United States, or the entire planet.

Know Your Charity

The best source of information about a charity is the charity itself. Take time to discover the individual success stories that make up a charity's work in its field. Try volunteering for one of its programs or tour its headquarters. Charities have an obligation to provide detailed information to interested donors. Never give to a charity you know nothing about. Request written literature and a copy of the charity's latest annual report. Honest charities typically encourage your interest and respond to your questions.

Find Out How Your Dollars Are Spent

Ask how much of your donation goes for general administration and fund-raising expenses and how much is left for the program services you want to support. The American Institute of Philanthropy's Charity Rating Guide recommends that sixty percent or more of your charitable donation should go to program services.

Do Not Respond to Pressure

Altruism and a desire to help are the best reasons for giving.

Do not be swayed by charities asking for your dollar through guilt and intimidation. Do not give to an unknown charity over the telephone, especially if it pressures you to give immediately or refuses to send information unless you make a pledge.

Keep Records of Your Donations

Never give cash. Never give your credit card number to a telephone solicitor you do not know. Give your gift by check or money order so you will have a record for tax purposes. The IRS requires that you obtain a receipt from the charity (a canceled check will not suffice) for all tax-deductible contributions of $250 or more.

Tax Exempt Versus Tax Deductible

"Tax exempt" and "tax deductible" are not synonymous phrases. Tax exempt means the organization does not have to pay taxes. Tax deductible means the donor can deduct contributions to the charity on his or her federal income tax return.

Do Not Be Misled by a Familiar Name

Some questionable charities use an impressive name that closely resembles the name of a respected, legitimate organization. Ask for information in writing. Check out the charity with AIP or other watchdogs, or check with your state charity registration office before making a contribution.

Beware of Charities Offering Gifts

Direct mail solicitations are often accompanied by greeting cards, address stickers, calendars, key rings or other "gifts." Charities do this because it can increase donations. Do not feel that you have to make a contribution to keep these "gifts."

It is against the law for a charity to demand payment for any unordered merchandise. Be aware that these enclosed items can mean higher fund-raising costs for the organization.

Check the Ratings

To check how a charity is rated, click the "ratings" button on any one of the web sites listed below. Remember that many of these sites track primarily national charities. To find out about local charities, contact your area Better Business Bureau or your state's Attorney General's Office for Consumer Affairs.

112

> *American Institute of Philanthropy*
> *(www.charitywatch.org)*
> *BBB Wise Giving Alliance (www.give.org)*
> *Better Business Bureau Philanthropic Advisory Service*
> *(www.bbb.org)*
> *Charity America (www.charityamerica.com)*
> *Exempt Organization Search (www.irs.ustreas.gov/*
> *prod/bus_info/eo/eosearch.html)*
> *GuideStar (www.guidestar.org)*
> *Philanthropy Search.com (www.philanthropy*
> *search.com)*

32 Support the Military

There is nothing so likely to produce peace as to be well prepared to meet an enemy.

—GEORGE WASHINGTON

FEW GENERATIONS IN OUR nation's history have been exempt from war. Certainly in the last one hundred years, at least six prolonged international conflicts have required military participation by the United States. Those who serve in the military are those who deserve our appreciation, recognition, and full support. Shortly before becoming secretary of state, Colin Powell wrote:

"The volunteer G.I.s of today stand watch in Korea, the Persian Gulf, Europe and the dangerous terrain of the Balkans. We must never see them as mere hirelings, off in a corner of our society. They are our best, and we owe them our full support and our sincerest thanks. . . .

"As this century closes, we look back to identify the great leaders and personalities of the past 100 years. We do so in a world still troubled, but full of promise. That promise was gained by the young men and women of America who fought and died for freedom. Near the top of any listing of the most important people of the 20th century must stand, in singular honor, the American G.I."

Enlist in the Military—the Ultimate Support

The foremost way to support the military, of course, is to enlist! To find out more about that possibility, contact a local recruiting office for the Air Force, Army, Coast Guard, Marine Corps, or Navy. These offices are nearly always listed in local telephone directories under the alphabetical listing of "Recruiting" in special government pages. Those who have been in the military may want to reactivate their "reserve" status. Many cities have reserve recruiting offices for just that purpose.

The local recruiting office can explain fully the options and career paths available to those who volunteer for the military, including ROTC programs and the full range of benefits (including scholarships, home loans, and retirement benefits).

Close Cousins to the Military

President Bush created the Department of Homeland Security following the September 11, 2001, terrorist attacks. There are four other government entities that are vitally concerned with the defense of Americans at home and abroad. You may want to consider pursuing a career with the Secret Service, the Federal Bureau of Investigation, the Central Intelligence Agency, or the U.S. State Department. Each of these entities has online information available through www.USBluePages.gov.

Participate in USO Activities

The United Service Organizations (USO) does far more than sponsor concerts to entertain overseas troops! Although it was chartered by Congress as a nonprofit charitable corporation, the USO is not a part of the government. It draws its financial support from thousands of individual and corporate donors. The USO mission is to provide morale, welfare, and recreation-type services to uniformed military personnel. It does this by extending a "touch of home" through 122 centers, including five mobile canteens, and overseas centers in twelve nations. More than thirty independent affiliated USO corporations are located throughout the United States. The USO serves more than five million patrons annually.

USO programs include "newcomer" briefings for troops and their families, cultural awareness seminars, airport service centers, family-oriented activities, children's programs, employment assistance to military personnel upon discharge, new-bride orientations, and telephone, internet, and email capabilities to help link military personnel to family and friends at home. You can volunteer your time to the USO, or you can make a financial contribution to help fund USO activities. Information about both volunteering and contributing is available on the USO web site at www.uso.com.

Support Individual Soldiers

Places of worship and civic groups often have names of individual soldiers they have "adopted" or who are members of their organizations (or have parents who are members). Soldiers are always eager to receive mail from home, especially mail that is encouraging and that shares tidbits of news about what is happening in a soldier's hometown community. Here are several practical ways you can help support an individual soldier:

★ Send a letter or email message saying, "Thank you for the service you are giving to our country. I'm thinking about you and I'm praying for you and your family."

★ Send a care package—perhaps a T-shirt from the soldier's favorite sports team or a box of snack foods that may not be available on an overseas base.

★ Take some pictures of the soldier's family (including family pets) and send the pictures to the soldier. Candid photos of loved ones are always welcome!

★ Make a tape of special messages from the soldier's family and friends. If you know the favorite radio station of a soldier, you may want to record an hour or so of radio music and talk and send it with a message, "Just wanted you to stay current with what's getting airtime at home!"

★ Visit a soldier's family to see if the family is in need—sometimes a soldier's spouse just needs somebody to talk to about his or her fears, concerns, and struggles. At times, you may find an opportunity to help care for the family in more practical ways.

33 Correspond with a Foreign Pen Pal

*A man's feet should be planted in his country,
but his eyes should survey the world.*

—GEORGE SANTAYANA

TRAVELING THE GLOBE as a goodwill ambassador is not an option for everyone. But becoming a pen pal turns any citizen into just that—an international goodwill ambassador!

You can be a shy person and still enjoy corresponding with a stranger halfway around the world. You don't need special clothes, education, or training. You don't have to meet a schedule or specific expectations. Yet you can make a friend for life and influence how both that person and the other people in your pen pal's life view America and Americans.

You don't have to have a computer or know a foreign language to be a good pen pal. All you need is an interest in people, a willingness to write about yourself, a curiosity about cultures other than your own, stationery, and postage!

People have been writing pen pals for many years. President Ronald Reagan began writing to a pen pal while he was in high school and he continued to correspond with her throughout his career as an actor, governor of California, and president of the United States.

The Basics of Correspondence

To successfully correspond with a person in another nation remember a few basic rules:

★ Be on your best behavior. Remember that most cultures are not as relaxed as ours. Slang and off-color jokes or words may be very offensive to your pal.

★ Begin your letters by inquiring about his or her life. Ask about the culture and try to discover how life is different or similar to your own. Show interest in your pal. Then share some basic things about yourself and your life in the United States.

★ Keep your sentences and concepts simple; your pal may be a novice at reading English.

★ Be prompt in responding to letters. You and your pal will develop a rhythm of how often you write. But never wait more than a month to respond to postal mail or a week for electronic mail (email).

★ Unless you and your pen pal chose one another based on a common interest in international affairs, avoid making opinionated statements about international politics. You can discuss, of course, how events are effecting your life and the lives of your family members.

★ A foreign pen pal is not the person to whom you should air your criticisms of American politics or policies.

Where to Find a Pen Pal

You can begin looking for a pen pal for yourself or your child in some familiar places. Your church's missionary organization may have lists of people around the globe waiting to connect with a pen pal. Likewise, you may call the guidance counselor at your child's school (or his or her teacher) to see if the school is already participating in a pen pal network. Organizations and civic clubs with international affiliates, such as Rotary and 4-H clubs, may also have pen pal lists.

You might also visit a web site that hosts pen pal information, such as www.ks-connection.org/penpal/penpal.html. This web site is set up specifically to match children with pen pals. Children may find pen pals from around the world in their own age groups.

Some sites connect people based on common interests. Christian Pen Pals (at www.Christianpenpals.com) allows you to connect with a Christian pen pal from the nation of your choice.

Some sites are created especially for educators who wish to enter their classes into a database in order to connect with other classrooms around the world:

★ *Email Classroom Exchange.* At www.epals.com, you'll not only find an ever growing database of classes, but you'll also find a conference room where your class can chat with your pen pal!

★ *Keypal Club.* Log on to www.teaching.com/keypals and fill out their database of information. Then you can search their database for a pen pal!

★ *SAPE.* Soviet-American Penpal Exchange matches people from the USA and other countries with pen pals in the former Soviet Union and the Baltic Nations. Visit www.michander.com.

★ *Web66: WWW School Registry.* Schools from around the world have registered their web sites here. Pick a region of the world, and mail them your request.

Note: Listings of web sites and resources for pen pals should not be construed as an endorsement of any service or information provided by these sites. Parents are encouraged to monitor their child's use of the internet.

120

34 Attend Intercultural Events

Peace and friendship with all mankind is our wisest policy, and I wish we may be permitted to pursue it.

—THOMAS JEFFERSON

ONE OF THE GREAT STRENGTHS of our nation is that people of so many different cultures have made the United States their home. In the early part of the twentieth century, the big cities of the United States had the greatest racial diversity. That is no longer the case. Now, small and medium-size towns and cities throughout the nation are also home to people of a variety of ethnic heritages.

People who are "different" or who are perceived as "not like me" can cause some people to be afraid. That fear is generally a fear of the unknown, and the best way to overcome it is to get to know someone who isn't like you! Here are some simple suggestions:

1. Take the initiative to welcome newcomers into your school or neighborhood and get to know them. Discuss their concerns. Very likely their concerns are the same as yours: good schools, safe neighborhoods, honest work with fair pay, affordable housing, access to good medical care, and an opportunity to advance educationally and economically. Do what you can to help newcomers find answers to the questions they ask or solve problems they face.

2. There are a number of holidays that will help you learn about other cultures. Take advantage of the opportunity to participate in the celebrations of various ethnic groups—for example:

★ Kwanzaa, an African-American heritage celebration

★ Chinese New Year, a spring festival featuring dragons, fireworks, and parades

★ St. Patrick's Day, an Irish festival in honor of a popular Christian saint

★ Cinco de Mayo, a Mexican celebration of independence day in Mexico

If none of these events are observed in your area, consider organizing a heritage festival in your school or town to learn about and celebrate other cultures.

3. Consider inviting an international student or students to visit in your home. Contact a local college or university to find out how you might get in touch with foreign students who would enjoy meeting an American family. Then, extend an invitation to your home or to a typically American restaurant or cultural experience (such as the County Fair or a baseball game). Be sure to pick up the tab for those you invite! Extending hospitality to people from other countries is a great way to learn more about other cultures and nations.

4. Organize a forum to establish or help develop lines of

communication between people of different cultures in your town or city. Select a topic that would be pertinent to people of all races, such as racism or discrimination.

5. Learn another language. It is probably some time since you studied foreign language in school, but it may be easier than you think to pick up that language again. Local schools and junior colleges often offer refresher courses to help people recall a language they once studied.

6. Teach English as a second language to non-English-speaking people who have moved into your town. Help them make the transition to a new country. There are many opportunities to be certified as a teacher, and many opportunities to teach.

Sing Your Patriotism

I know only two tunes: one of them is "Yankee Doodle," and the other isn't.

—ULYSSES S. GRANT

EVEN THOSE WHO CANNOT SING well *can* enjoy expressing their patriotism in song! Learning the stories behind some of our most famous patriotic songs can add to the feelings of patriotism as you sing.

Here is a brief introduction to four of our most beloved national songs.

The Star-Spangled Banner

During the War of 1812, on September 13, 1814, Francis Scott Key visited the British fleet in Chesapeake Bay to secure the release of Dr. William Beanes, who had been captured after the burning of Washington, D.C. The release was secured, but Key was detained on ship overnight during the shelling of Fort McHenry, one of the forts defending Baltimore. In the morning, he was so delighted to see the American flag still flying over the fort that he began a poem to commemorate the occasion.

Entitled "The Star Spangled Banner," the poem soon attained wide popularity as sung to the tune "To Anacreon in Heaven." The origin of this tune is not known.

"The Star-Spangled Banner" was officially made the national anthem by Congress in 1931, although it had already been adopted as such by the Army and Navy.

You're a Grand Old Flag

Broadway producer, playwright, and actor George M. Cohan was frequently inspired by headlines and news from the front during World War II. In 1906, Cohan starred in his production titled "George Washington Jr." In one scene, he marched up and down the stage carrying an American flag while singing a song titled: "You're a Grand Old Rag." When opposition was voiced to the title, Cohan renamed the tune to "You're a Grand Old Flag." This scene from Broadway was later memorialized in a movie starring James Cagney titled *Yankee Doodle Dandy*—a dramatization of Cohan's life based on his autobiography by the same title.

America the Beautiful

Katharine Lee Bates, a minister's daughter and long-time professor at Wellesley College, was lecturing at the summer session at Colorado College when she joined an expedition to the summit of Pikes Peak in a prairie wagon. "It was then and there," she wrote, as she "was looking out over the sea-like expanse" that she hastily scribbled into a notebook four stanzas of what later became "America the Beautiful." The words first appeared in print in a weekly periodical on July 4, 1895.

The only payment Miss Bates ever received for her efforts was a small check from that periodical.

Bates later rewrote some of the lyrics, and the new version was published in the *Boston Evening Transcript* on November 19, 1904.

In 1926, the National Federation of Music Clubs held a contest to put the poem to music, but none of the entries was deemed suitable. The poem has been sung to a variety of music, and Miss Bates never admitted publicly which music she liked best. Today, "America the Beautiful" is almost exclusively sung to Samuel A. Ward's "Materna."

126

Also in 1926, a strong push was made to adopt the hymn as the national anthem. But the older, more established "Star-Spangled Banner" won official status in 1931. Even today, however, advocates of Bates' hymn continue to lobby for official anthem status.

God Bless America

Often considered one of America's unofficial national anthems, "God Bless America" was composed by an immigrant, Irving Berlin, who left his home in Siberia for America when he was only five years old. The original version of "God Bless America" was written by Berlin during the summer of 1918 at Camp Upton, located in Yaphank, Long Island, for his Ziegfeld-style revue titled "Yip, Yip, Yaphank." Berlin decided, however, that the solemn tone of "God Bless America" was somewhat out of keeping with the more comedic elements of the show and the song was laid aside.

In the fall of 1938, as war again threatened Europe, Berlin decided to write a "peace" song. He recalled his "God Bless America" from twenty years earlier and made some alterations to reflect the different state of the world. Singer Kate Smith introduced the revised "God Bless America" during her radio broadcast on Armistice Day in 1938. The song was an immediate hit. Berlin soon established the God Bless America Fund, dedicating the royalties to the Boy and Girl Scouts of America.

Why Not Sing Along?

You will find the words to most of these anthems in appendix D. You might also enjoy going to the web site www.treefort.org/~rgrogan/web/flagmusic.htm to listen to the music for each of these songs. Go ahead and sing along!

When you sing patriotic songs, don't worry about high notes, low notes, or even out-of-tune notes. Just sing with the conviction of the words, give thanks in your heart that they are true, and pay tribute to those whose sacrifices made it so.

36 Participate in a Community Drive

I like to see a man proud of the place in which he lives. I like to see a man who lives in it so that his place will be proud of him.

—ABRAHAM LINCOLN

BLOOD DRIVE. FOOD DRIVE. United Way fund drive. Toy drive. Winter coats drive. There are numerous "drives" that benefit your community. Get involved! If you see an unmet need in your community, choose to do something about it. Here are some tips to help organize a blood drive for a community, but you can use some of the same concepts for a drive of any type. In our example of a blood drive, the local Red Cross blood center or bloodmobile can staff your donation site. Your job would be to recruit donors and encourage participation. In other cases, an established agency may be able to provide a great deal of help. Start by contacting the foremost agency related to the need you perceive, and learn how you can plug into existing efforts.

Develop a Timetable for the Drive

Any kind of community drive takes coordination and organization to be successful. First, list all of the tasks that need to be done, from recruiting volunteers to sending publicity notices to writing follow-up thank-you notes. Then, develop a timeline—start at the proposed date of your event and work backward to the present date making sure that all tasks are given sufficient time and staffing.

Recruit a Team or Committee

129

To be really effective you need a group or committee. If you are already part of a group such as a Kiwanis Club or Lions Club, you already have a great organization in place to lend support for a worthy cause. If you don't belong to a civic organization, perhaps you are part of an informal group, such as a women's Bible study or an exercise group. Poll your friends to see if they are interested in helping. A group that already has some natural cohesion can be energized by taking on a cause. Your enthusiasm is your best recruitment tool. Your committee will be energized by your energy.

Contact Donors

Enlist new prospects even as you contact donors from past drives. Work with the Red Cross to get names of people who have donated blood in the past and contact them to set up appointments. Donors with confirmed appointments are more likely to participate. You can enlist new prospects by promoting your event through public service announcements, fliers, and the most effective way—word of mouth.

Get the Word Out

A blood drive is not a hard cause to promote; it is a cause that everyone can appreciate. So get the word out.

Ask youth groups from places of worship or schools to deliver publicity fliers to local merchants and request that they display the fliers in their store windows. Contact service clubs or businesses to encourage their members or employees to donate blood. The student council of your local high school can recruit teachers and students who are at least seventeen years of age to donate. Invite physicians to post fliers in their offices. Recruit service organizations and religious groups to make calls and get notices to their membership. Local merchants may be willing to support the drive by providing refreshments and recruiting entertainment.

You might also print mini-fliers to be mailed with bank or utility statements. Distribute announcements for publication in worship bulletins and service club newsletters. Find related stories with a human-interest angle to be reported in the local newspaper. Make public service announcements and be available for interviews on the radio. Get on the agenda of clubs or organization meetings and make presentations of the need and background of the blood drive.

Generate Enthusiasm

Get local leaders and "celebrities" to help promote the blood drive. Ask the mayor, community leader or elected official to proclaim a Volunteer Blood Donor Appreciation Day. Invite local politicians or celebrities to donate, and contact the local media to cover the event. Set a goal for sign-ups and post a progress report on the main street of your town to show how close you are to reaching your goal.

Be Informed

Some people may have fears about donating blood. Dispel misunderstanding about blood donations with the facts. Find out how much blood is needed to ensure that your town has an adequate supply. Publicize donor eligibility guidelines.

Assign Volunteers to Help at the Donation Center

On the day(s) of your event, volunteers will be needed to register donors, serve refreshments, and call donors who missed appointments.

Cater to services your donors may need so they can participate in the blood drive. For instance, baby-sitters and face-painters might be recruited to entertain young children while their parents are donating blood.

Follow Through with Thanks and Evaluation

Saying "thank you" and showing appreciation is essential. A personal, one-on-one word of thanks is most effective. Sponsor an appreciation luncheon or coffee for your volunteers. Give an award to the volunteer who recruited the most donors. Contact the local news with the results of the drive. Ask those involved what could be done differently to make the event better. Keep records and notes from the drive to help organize a future event. Remove fliers and signs used to publicize the event.

The great thing about a community drive is that it builds community spirit by allowing everyone to get involved, and at the same time it provides real help to citizens in need.

37 Understand and Obey the Law

A real patriot is the fellow who gets a parking ticket and rejoices that the system works.

—BILL VAUGHN

CHECK ANY THESAURUS and you'll find the following words associated with the concept of freedom: liberty, liberation, unfettered, open, unhampered, autonomous, emancipated, independent, self-governing, self-ruling, bounteous, bountiful, charitable, eager, generous, hospitable, lavish, open-handed, redeemed.

Look up the word "tyranny" and you'll find words such as these: arbitrary control, autocratic, cruel, despotic, dictatorial, domineering, high-handed, oppressive, overbearing, authoritarian, coercion, unreasonableness, unjustness.

Americans choose to live in a world ordered by the first set of words associated with freedom!

For freedom to exist between two or more people, however, two related concepts need to be in place:

★ *Restriction.* No person can live in absolute freedom. As the old adage goes, "Your freedom to swing your fist ends at my nose." Some rule of law needs to be in place for two people to enjoy maximum freedom in *relationship* to each other.

★ *Reciprocity.* Perhaps the oldest rule of law known to mankind is the law of reciprocity: "Do unto others as you would have them do unto you." While this law is not stated in the statutes of any nation, it nevertheless has enjoyed universal appeal for thousands of years: "Don't steal my goat and I won't steal yours"; "Don't encroach on my territory and I won't encroach on yours"; "Don't take my spouse and I won't take yours."

For restrictive laws to work in reciprocity, all parties involved must obey the laws.

Obey the Law

Ideally, obedience to the law is voluntary. Teach your children to voluntarily obey the law by doing the following:

★ Model personal obedience to the law. Drive within the speed limit and follow seatbelt and child-restraint safety laws. Pay your taxes on time. Don't call in sick when you are not. Don't litter.

Not all laws are legal statutes—some are simply agreed-upon cultural "rules." Regardless of the origin or penalties associated with a law, keep it! Set an example of obedience.

★ Make sure that you express family rules clearly. The best time to state family rules is *before* they are tested, not after. At times, specific rules may need to be stated—for example, before entering a store or amusement park. Ask your children to repeat your rule back to you to make sure they understand what behavior is expected.

★ Rules are best kept when they are understood and are rooted in common sense. Explain to your children as fully as possible *why* certain rules and laws have been established. Point out the benefits that come from having laws and obeying them.

★ Require that your children obey you as a parent, especially when rules are related to their safety, health, or the moral virtues your family values. Clearly state just and fair consequences for disobeying family rules and enforce them with equality. At the same time, hold out rewards for obedience and give them generously.

★ Point out to your children ways in which a rule of law works for their practical benefit. For example: Leaving the house at the established time allows you to avoid detention at school!

★ From time to time, conduct a family discussion using Robert's Rules of Order or formal debate rules. Allow your children to see firsthand that respectful use of *words* can result in mutually beneficial solutions and decisions.

Changing the Law

Obey the law even if you don't agree with a law. Two of the great strengths of America are that we allow for the orderly and peaceful change of law, and that average citizens can be involved in the process of legal change through elections and communication with elected officials. If you don't like an existing law, say so through the appropriate channels and to the right people.

Recognize that the democratic political process is one rooted in compromise and that the changes you seek in the law may need to be amended to accommodate the changes others desire.

You can teach your children these basic principles through simple measures:

★ Allow your children to see you communicate with your elected officials. If appropriate, invite your children to write their own letter or to make your letter a family letter with all in the family signing it. Writing out a suggestion for change often helps a person to clarify what he or she truly believes, as well as helps a child to develop a point of view that he or she can state clearly.

★ Allow your children the freedom to voice their dislike for a family rule. There should be no penalty or punishment for *voicing* disagreement in a respectful manner. Whenever possible— specifically, in cases involving style, opinion, or preference—be willing to compromise. Consider your children's point of view. Talk through the issue. Reach a workable solution that is agreeable to everyone. At the same time, express to your children that because you are *responsible* for them, you bear the ultimate *authority* over them. In the end, your will as a parent is the deciding factor.

★ When discussing political issues with your children, point out the need for compromise. No political party, no president, and no point of view has its way all the time. What is true in the halls of Congress is also true on the playground and in social clubs.

135

38 Voice Respect for Authority

We aspire to nothing that belongs to others. We seek no dominion over our fellow man, but man's dominion over tyranny and misery.

—LYNDON B. JOHNSON

NOT ALL AUTHORITY FIGURES are elected officials or civic workers. Certainly all parents know they have authority over their own children. Grandparents and other family members, teachers, principals, and even playground and crosswalk monitors are also likely to exert authority over your children at some point. Religious leaders, community leaders, and at times, medical professionals can also be authority figures. Showing respect for those in authority is a vital part of manifesting and teaching respect for the rule of law.

Law and Order

The words "law and order" are often put together because law creates order. Law is rooted in words and symbols; it is an intangible expression of desire. The order created by the enactment of law, however, is tangible, concrete, and practical. Teach your children the relationship between law and order, and the benefits of order, by doing the following:

★ Choose to live in an orderly fashion. Insist that your children pick up their own messes and clean up their own spills. Set family rules that give an order to time, space, and group activities.

★ Voice your appreciation and respect for those in authority. Teach your children to address authority figures in a polite and courteous way. The use of "Yes, sir," and "No, ma'am" are still appropriate for children in the twenty-first century!

★ Point out to your children the practical way in which laws or rules govern fair play. Every sport is played according to rules, and those who play by the rules are always winners when it comes to sportsmanship. Voice your appreciation for the good sportsmanship your children display in playing with others.

Dealing with Rebellion

Those who rebel against authority figures nearly always do themselves harm emotionally and socially. They can also cause harm to both people and property—which is where rebellion becomes an act of disobeying the law. If you fear that your child is in danger of disobeying the law, consider making a trip to juvenile court as observers. Also consider taking your child—and perhaps his or her Scout troop, religion-based group, or social group—to visit a prison. Let your child see firsthand the consequences of lawbreaking.

A number of community projects use prison labor—such as picking up litter and scrubbing graffiti from public property—and some of these projects allow participation by com-

137

munity volunteers. Consider spending a Saturday working alongside these prisoners as a family. Let your child see first-hand the meaning of the term "hard labor." Preventing law-breaking is easier and more beneficial than dealing with the consequences.

Manifesting Respect

Here are some ways you can teach your children to show re-spect for all who are in authority:

138

★ Teach your children to stand up when adults enter a room.

★ Teach your children to open doors and pull out chairs to help seat others.

★ Teach your children how to give firm handshakes and to look people in the eyes as they give compliments.

★ Explain to your children why you pull to one side of the road to allow a funeral procession to pass; why you take off your hat in a place of worship, as you sing the national an-them, or say the Pledge of Allegiance; and why you refer to various professionals as "your honor," "doctor," "reverend," or "counselor." Give a reason for the respect you have for those who fill positions of honor and authority.

39 Accept Jury Duty Gladly

The only thing that has ever distinguished America among the nations is that she has shown that all men are entitled to the benefits of law.

—WOODROW WILSON

THROUGH LAW AND CUSTOM, safeguards have been developed in the United States to assure that people accused of wrongdoing will be treated fairly. One of those safeguards is the right to a trial by jury, which is guaranteed in the U.S. Constitution. The rights of an accused person are set forth in the Sixth Amendment. These include the right to "a speedy and public trial." The right to a speedy trial means that a person must be tried as soon as possible after being accused. The right to a public trial means a defendant cannot be tried in secret. Each trial must be open to public observation.

Fair treatment also means charges against the accused will be heard and judged by a jury of his or her peers. A trial by jury is one of the most basic rights of American citizens, and jury duty is one of the most basic responsibilities of American citizenship.

Jurors play an essential role in the American justice system in guaranteeing a citizen's rights. Without jurors, the judicial system as provided in the Constitution cannot work the way the authors intended.

Who Can and Cannot Serve as Jurors

140

The courts select names of possible jurors from sources such as the tax rolls and voting lists. From those names, people are then summoned for possible service on a jury. Before becoming a jury member, a person is questioned by the trial judge, the opposing lawyers, or both.

United States citizens over the age of eighteen who reside in the county that issued the jury summons and are able to understand the English language are eligible to serve on a jury.

People who have been convicted of a felony offense are not permitted to serve.

The Constitution of the United States provides that jurors in a criminal trial must be neutral regarding the case. In most situations, the jurors are selected from the community where the crime occurred. An accused person may choose to be tried by a judge without a jury.

If You Receive a Summons

Recognize that serving on a jury is rarely "convenient." Jury duty often requires that schedules be rearranged, appointments canceled, and work missed. On the positive side, those who serve on a jury usually find it to be a personally rewarding experience. It is both an opportunity to learn about the judicial system firsthand and an opportunity to serve. In fact, jury service is often the most direct participation an average citizen has in the working of government.

If you receive a jury summons, follow the instructions on the summons to appear in the court when you are requested to be there. If you are unable to serve during the time requested on the summons, you may contact the jury office and ask for a postponement of your service until a later date. If you have serious hardship, you may be excused from jury duty for up to a year. Your employer must allow you time off to serve on a jury.

In spite of the inconvenience to private citizens, jury duty is a privilege. Not every country protects its citizens with jury trials. Many nondemocratic governments claim to protect the rights of their citizens, but in practice, they do so only when they find it politically convenient.

Your willingness to serve on a jury and to give the accused a fair and impartial hearing is one essential way you can stand up for America by helping to protect the rights of its citizens. Give someone else the fair treatment you would want for yourself in the same situation.

40

Honor Our Veterans

142

And they who for their country die shall fill an honored grave, for glory lights the soldier's tomb, and beauty weeps the brave.

—JOSEPH DRAKE

TWO NATIONAL HOLIDAYS are a prime time to honor those who have rendered military service to our nation. Full participation in these holidays is an excellent expression of patriotism:

★ *Veterans Day.* In 1921, an unknown World War I American soldier was buried in Arlington National Cemetery on a hillside overlooking the Potomac River and the city of Washington. A similar ceremony occurred in England and France. These memorial gestures all took place on November 11, giving universal recognition to the celebrated ending of World War I fighting at eleven o'clock in the morning on November 11, 1918 (11th hour of the 11th day of the 11th month).

"Armistice Day" was the name given to this holiday in

1926 by a congressional resolution. The name was given in the idealistic hope that World War I was the "war to end all wars." It became a national holiday twelve years later by similar congressional action. Just a few years after the holiday was proclaimed, however, war broke out in Europe. In 1954, President Eisenhower signed a bill proclaiming November 11 as "Veterans Day"—a day to honor *all* who have served America in *all* wars.

In commemoration of Veterans Day, official national ceremonies are held at the Tomb of the Unknowns in Arlington National Cemetery. A combined color guard presents arms, tribute is paid by the laying of a presidential wreath, and a bugler plays taps. These ceremonies are coordinated by the President's Veterans Day National Committee, which represents several national veterans organizations. On a local level, parades and special ceremonies are often held to honor veterans in the community.

You can commemorate this day by attending Veterans Day parades. Applaud those who have served in the military. On a personal level, Veterans Day is an excellent time to send a note to someone you know who served in the military. Say simply, "Thanks for defending the freedom I value highly."

★ *Memorial Day.* Three years after the Civil War ended, on May 5, 1868, the head of an organization of former Union soldiers and sailors established Decoration Day as a time for the nation to decorate the graves of the war dead with flowers. Major General John A. Logan designated May 30 as the date of annual remembrance. Approximately twenty-five places in both the North and South have been named in connection with the origin of Memorial Day. By the end of the nineteenth century, Memorial Day ceremonies were being held on May 30 across the nation; many state legislatures passed proclamations designating the day and the Army and Navy both adopted regulations for proper observance at their facilities. It was not until after World War I, however, that the day was expanded to honor all who died in all American wars. In 1971, Memorial Day was declared a national holiday and the date was adjusted to fall on the last Monday in May.

While Veterans Day is a time of celebration and honor, Memorial Day is a time of remembrance and honor. Both flags and flowers are appropriately placed on the graves of those who died in war.

Visit a local cemetery on Memorial Day and lay a wreath or a bouquet of flowers on the gravesite of a soldier. Take your children with you. Express your gratitude for those who willingly gave their lives for the freedom we enjoy today. Say a prayer for their families and heirs who are still alive.

Help a Veteran in Need

Many who have served our nation in military service are in need of help. Get the information you need to help them, or direct them to help. The Department of Veterans Affairs, accessed at http://www.VA.gov, is an excellent place to get information related to vocational rehabilitation, home loans, educational benefits, life insurance and pension benefit programs, and appeals to the Board of Veterans' Appeals. Information is also provided about special programs to help homeless, minority, and women veterans.

Other Ways to Honor Veterans

Consider one of these four additional ways of honoring veterans:

★ Invite a veteran to lunch or dinner with your family. Include his or her spouse. Ask the veteran to tell your children what it was like in our nation at the time he volunteered or was drafted for service. The veteran need not be asked to share details of wartime experience, but should be encouraged to tell how he *felt* about serving and about returning to civilian life after serving. You may ask what it was like to live and serve in the military while overseas or in another state.

★ Visit a nearby military cemetery or memorial honoring those who served our nation. From park statues to plaques hung in lobbies to memorials to veterans and to those killed in war abroad—take note of them.

★ Plan a visit to the National Veterans Museum. Currently under construction, this museum will open in Washington, D.C., in 2004.

★ Take a bouquet of flowers to a veteran's hospital and ask that the flowers be given to a soldier who hasn't received any flowers, or perhaps that they be placed in a central lobby area. You might want to do this in honor or memory of a family member who served in the military.

145

41 Learn about Pending Legislation

Our country, right or wrong. When right, to be kept right; when wrong, to be put right.

—CARL SCHURZ

LITERALLY DOZENS OF BILLS and resolutions are processed by Congress every session. Do you know the ones pending a vote this month? Part of being a member of the informed electorate means knowing as much as possible about candidates for public office and issues that are brought to a public vote. It also means being informed about what your representatives are currently doing in the U.S. House of Representatives and U.S. Senate.

Three Key Sources of Information

Three outstanding sources of information about pending legislation and the legislative process are listed below and are available on the internet. For those who don't have computers, internet access is nearly always available at your local public library.

★ *Thomas Legislative Information.* This unbiased, objective forum is presented "in the spirit of Thomas Jefferson." It is a service of the Library of Congress and can be accessed at http://thomas.loc.gov or through www.congress.gov. The web site provides current information about pending legislation, the congressional record of bills passed and the voting related to them, and committee information for both the House and Senate. You can gain detailed information about each bill and its progress through the political maze to the time of vote.

Specific areas highlight legislation related to current issues (such as the attack on America September 11, 2001) and long-standing issues (such as the future of Medicare and appropriations bills). Various historical documents can be accessed through this site, as well as information about how the legislative process works.

★ *U.S. Senate.* The web site for the United States Senate, accessed at http://www.senate.gov, gives the daily agenda for the Senate, as well as a monthly schedule of bills and resolutions pending discussion, debate, and vote. Brief descriptions of each bill and resolution are provided on the monthly calendar; specific information can be accessed using a bill's number or by conducting a keyword search.

★ *U.S. House of Representatives.* The web site for the United States House of Representatives, accessed through http://www.house.gov, gives a weekly schedule of legislation and resolutions "for possible consideration." As is also true for the Senate web site, membership on committees is provided, as well as various educational links to help a person become better acquainted with the political process.

Both the Senate and House web sites provide information about how to contact your elected representatives.

Other Sources of Information

Valuable insight into various levels of legislation can be obtained by doing the following:

★ *Reading your local newspaper.* City, county, and state issues pending legislation are likely to be presented on both the news pages and editorial pages of your local newspaper.

★ *Reading or listening to political commentary.* A number of news and politically oriented magazines, radio programs, and television programs present both factual information and commentary related to the legislative and political process. Find your favorite sources of information and read or listen regularly.

★ *Watching C-Span.* Live proceedings of Congress, including key hearings, speeches, and debates, are available on the C-Span channel available via cable television and direct-access TV to millions of viewers across America.

★ *Reading internet statements posted by the Republican and Democratic National Committees.* The web sites of the Republican and Democratic political parties include commentary on key legislation, as well as information about how to voice your opinion to your elected representatives.

Those who stay informed about legislation are far more likely to become active in the political process. What you don't know *can* impact your life in negative and positive ways. Seek both to know and participate in the processes that shape your life and the life of the nation.

42

Read about Sacrifices for Freedom

And so, my fellow Americans: ask not what your country can do for you—ask what you can do for your country.

—JOHN F. KENNEDY

THE STRANGE THING ABOUT FREEDOM is that those who sacrifice most to secure it often don't live to enjoy it. Few Americans grasp the depth of sacrifice made willingly by thousands of people on our behalf. While we can never really thank those who have sacrificed their lives, we can honor them by learning what they did and why.

A History of Sacrifice

Sadly, some people seem intent on editing history to make it more acceptable at the expense of the truth. The ease of accessing information via technology is accompanied by the ease of accepting misinformation. It's up to each one of us to find out the truth before unwittingly passing along incorrect information. Read. Ask questions. Learn more about sources of information before accepting as true everything you read or hear.

To read actual historical documents and records from the founding of our country until today, visit the National Archives and Records Administration (NARA) in person, through a public library, or online at www.nara.gov. NARA has libraries in eighteen states and the District of Columbia. In addition, short biographies of every signer of the Declaration of Independence may be read at www.colonialhall.com.

Examples Worthy of Remembrance

In a 1988 speech, Senator John McCain recalled a young man named Mike Christian who was placed in a cell with him and thirty to forty other prisoners of the North Vietnamese in 1971. Mike came from a small town near Selma, Alabama. He didn't wear a pair of shoes until he was thirteen years old. At seventeen, he enlisted in the United States Navy. He later earned a commission and became a Naval flying officer. Mike was shot down and captured in 1967.

McCain said, "Mike had a keen and deep appreciation for the opportunities this country—and our military—provide for people who want to work and want to succeed."

Mike managed to find enough bits of thread and torn clothing to fashion an American flag using a needle he made from bamboo. It took him a couple of months to complete his project and sew the American flag on the inside of his shirt.

"Every afternoon, before we had a bowl of soup, we would hang Mike's shirt on the wall of our cell, and say the Pledge of Allegiance," McCain said. "I know that saying the Pledge of Allegiance may not seem the most important or meaningful part of our day now. But I can assure you that—for those men in that stark prison cell—it was indeed the most important and meaningful event of our day."

Eventually the Vietnamese discovered Mike's shirt with the flag sewn inside, and they confiscated it. They beat Mike Christian severely for the next couple of hours in front of his fellow prisoners. When the soldiers left, Mike's friends tried to bind his wounds the best they could.

"After things quieted down, I went to lie down to go to sleep. As I did, I happened to look in the corner of the room. Sitting there beneath that dim light bulb, with a piece of white cloth, a piece of red cloth, another shirt and his bamboo needle, was my friend Mike Christian. He was sitting there, with his eyes almost shut from his beating, making another American flag. He was not making that flag because it made Mike Christian feel better. He was making that flag because he knew how important it was for us to be able to pledge our allegiance to our flag and our country."

Stories such as that of Mike Christian are not only inspiring to read or hear, but they are worthy of emulation in our own lives. Ask yourself and your family today:

1. What might we do to show our appreciation for our nation, even if others do not agree with us?

2. What sacrifices are we willing to make to strengthen our nation?

Share What You Learn

When you read an inspiring story about someone who sacrificed for our freedom, or perhaps someone who sacrificed a great deal in order to get to the United States to enjoy our freedoms, share the inspiration!

★ Pass the messages of sacrifices for freedom on to your friends via email or as enclosures to letters.

★ Post the messages on a department bulletin board, or suggest they be included in an office newsletter—especially if the article relates to the experiences of your company's employees.

★ Read the messages aloud to your family at the dinner table, or perhaps at a Thanksgiving Day meal. And then, add your own expressions of thanksgiving for those who have made the sacrifices that preserve our freedom and inspire our patriotism.

43 Write a Letter to the Editor

A government for the people must depend for its success on the intelligence, the morality, the justice, and the interest of the people themselves.

—GROVER CLEVELAND

ALETTER TO THE EDITOR is the modern-day equivalent of a soapbox in the town square. It is a way for the average citizen to express his or her views to the widest possible audience and to challenge fellow citizens to see an issue in a new light. It is also a forum that is almost completely unique to the free world, and as such it is a wonderful way to exercise your patriotism.

Almost all local and national newspapers and magazines invite public response to articles and events of interest to their readers. Most publications welcome a variety of signed letters that cover all points of view, particularly those that disagree with opinions expressed by the publication itself. Controversy, however, is not a requirement for getting a letter published.

The Best Time to Write

The best time to write a letter to the editor is when you find yourself mentally responding strongly to an article or issue. If you can't take time to write at that moment, tear out the article and jot down a few notes to help you get started later. It isn't necessary to be an expert on an issue to address it in print.

Guidelines for Getting a Letter Published

154

Here are some simple guidelines for gaining access to the "public soapbox":

★ Look in your newspaper for the postal address, fax number, or email address for letters to the editor, and note any additional instructions or guidelines.

★ When you write, respond to a recent article, editorial or op-ed, current issue or event, or offer a timely observation about a community need. If you are responding to a printed article, be sure to name the article and the date it appeared.

★ Don't address more than one issue or attempt to make more than one point.

★ Keep your letter simple, short, and clear—no more than three or four short paragraphs. Most newspapers limit submissions to 200–250 words. Editors usually reserve the right to edit letters to fit the space available. Letters that make a strong point without repetition or wordiness are less likely to be edited.

★ Be reasonable but don't be afraid to be direct, engaging, and personal.

★ Avoid attacking individuals (even if they are public figures) or groups. Deal with ideas, policies, and values.

★ Most publications avoid publishing poetry and letters that only serve to thank an individual or group.

★ Avoid making broad, sweeping statements that beg for proof. Use statistics sparingly or not at all. Always quote sources if statistics are important to your point (for example, "according to the *Wall Street Journal…*").

★ Ask another person to read your letter before you send it to see if you succeeded in clearly and effectively making your point.

★ Make sure your information is accurate.

★ Proofread your letter carefully before submitting it. Then have someone else proofread it again!

★ Always include your name, address, telephone number (and email address if that is how you submit the letter). An editor may call you to confirm that you wrote the letter and want it published. Be sure to let the editor know if you prefer that your full address not be published with your letter and name.

What Keeps a Letter from Being Published?

A letter is almost always doomed if it is too long, needs too much editing, isn't clear, has illegible handwriting, or addresses the same issue as many other letters already printed.

National Forums

Your local newspaper isn't the only forum in which to express your opinion. Consider writing a letter to a favorite newsmagazine, trade or professional paper, or newspaper in the town where you grew up or went to college. Be sure to establish your connection with that town early in your letter.

If you have access to the internet, you can find a link to thousands of newspapers in America and around the world at www.onlinenewspapers.com. Look for a link on the newspaper's page that refers to "letters to the editor," "opinions," or "editorials" to obtain the requirements for submitting letters.

Don't Be Discouraged

Don't be discouraged if your letter isn't published right away, or ever. Most newspapers hold letters until they have several on the same subject and then publish them in the same issue. It is not unusual to wait three to six weeks to see a letter published. Don't feel personally rejected if your letter isn't published. Take satisfaction in the fact that at least one editor or writer at the publication read your opinion!

Be Committed to Your Opinion

Finally, remember that a letter to the editor, like the soapbox in the town square, is a venue for personal declaration. Your message will be read by friends and foes alike, so be certain that your position is one to which you are solidly committed. Once an opinion is in print, it's difficult to retract it or to alter it in a way that will reach precisely the same audience.

44 Be Alert to Danger

Eternal vigilance is the condition, not only of liberty, but of everything which as civilized men we hold dear.

—AUGUST HECKSCHER

EVEN BEFORE SEPTEMBER 11, 2001—the day when most Americans became acutely aware of terrorist threats to our way of life on a large scale—life in America was not as safe as it was twenty years ago. Communities where crime was nearly unheard of only a few years ago are now finding it necessary to investigate every kind of crime imaginable including murder and gang activities.

The answer to protecting your life, family, and possessions begins with *not* fearing an attack. Instead, arm yourself with information and mental preparation for scenarios you hope will never occur. Furthermore, teach your family to be vigilant and careful, but not afraid. Begin by learning all you can about the areas where you, your family, your neighborhood, and your country are most vulnerable. Learn what steps can be taken to heighten your awareness of danger and reduce the possibility that danger will find an opportunity to play out. Then join with other individuals and groups to form a stronger network of security around your home and family.

Personal Safety

Here are some things that you can do to enhance your personal safety:

★ Don't venture into new neighborhoods on foot after dark unless you are with at least three other people.

★ If the parking lot or sidewalk of your workplace is poorly lit, ask your employer to install better lighting, especially if you must come to work early or leave after dark.

★ Walk at a brisk pace with your head up; be alert to your surroundings. Be cautious about making direct eye contact or speaking to strangers you pass on relatively deserted city streets.

★ Lock your car *any* time you leave it—especially if you are just letting it warm up in the winter. Lock all doors once you're in your car.

★ When alone in a strange city, wear clothing that does not attract attention. Leave flashy jewelry and other expensive accessories at home.

★ Be alert to what is happening around you, especially in crowds. Keep valuables zipped into a purse or case that you carry under your arm or in a buttoned pocket. Never carry valuables in a backpack or rear-facing fanny pack.

★ Try never to work alone in a deserted building, especially at night. If you must, lock yourself in your area and call a security guard or a person you know to escort you out of the building when you leave.

★ Have an emergency response number programmed into your phone and practice accessing it in the dark.

In Your Community

Here are suggestions to keep your home and neighborhood safe:

★ Form a neighborhood watch group. Ask your local police department to speak to your neighborhood group about how to set up the group and make it work.

★ Learn the evacuation procedures for your city in case of emergency. Think about potential terrorist targets in your area and discover what precautions are being taken to keep them secure.

★ Have a family emergency escape plan. Go over the plan in a family meeting and have fire drills twice a year.

★ Teach your children never to open the door to someone you have not said may enter your home. Keep a short list of people they may admit, such as family members and selected neighbors.

★ Meet your neighbors. Let them know your normal schedule and find out about theirs. Let your neighbors know when you will be away for several days.

★ Never open the door to strangers (day or night) who are not clearly identified. If you are alone, don't admit unexpected visitors even if they identify themselves.

★ Teach children to remain at school if their ride home does not show up and to go to a teacher or principal for help.

★ Never give your security door codes for home or work to anyone else. If you live in an apartment with a buzzer to admit people at the main door, tell strangers that you will come down to meet them in the lobby (a semipublic place where you can see them before you admit them).

★ Do not use ATMs in deserted areas, even if you are in a car.

★ Shield your credit card, pin number, and other personal codes from the view of others when you are using them.

★ Keep your spare house key in a place that is out of sight of the road and sidewalk.

45   Get Involved in a Political Party

The unity of freedom has never relied on the uniformity of opinion.

—JOHN F. KENNEDY

GETTING INVOLVED in a political party is a way of helping ensure that the people *you* want to represent *you* in government are elected to office. It is also an excellent way to learn more about political issues and processes, and to form your own political beliefs (as opposed to the political beliefs you may have been taught by others). Ultimately, the democratic political process is about people and ideas. Political parties concern themselves with both.

You can gain valuable insight into the two major political parties on the internet by accessing their web sites:

★ *RNC.* The Republican National Committee can be accessed at http://www.rnc.org or www.gop.com.

★ *DNC.* The Democratic National Committee can be accessed at http://democrats.org.

Both of these political party web sites give historical information about their respective parties, as well as information about current political leaders from the party, party symbols, election platforms, official party oaths, and convention rules. Party leadership and information about state party organizations are included, as well as information about how to contribute to each party.

Be Informed about the Role of Political Parties

We are so accustomed to hearing about Republicans and Democrats that we rarely pause to consider that these two parties were not always the main political parties in America. The first two parties were the Whigs (later known as the Federalists) and the Democratic-Republicans (founded in 1792 as a congressional caucus to fight for the Bill of Rights). Thomas Jefferson was the founder of the Democratic-Republican party and ironically, both the Democratic and Republican parties of today claim him as their philosophical founder.

In the aftermath of the election of John Quincy Adams in 1824—a highly contested election that resulted in a four-way split among Democratic-Republicans—Andrew Jackson emerged as a powerful political figure. Under his leadership, the Jacksonian Democrats won the presidency in 1828 and 1832. In 1844, the National Convention simplified the party's name to the Democratic Party.

The Republican Party was born in the early 1850s in the years preceding the Civil War. It was founded primarily by antislavery activists and individuals who believed the government should grant western lands to settlers free of charge. John Charles Fremont was the first nominee for president in 1856 under the slogan, "Free soil, free labor, free speech, free men, Fremont." As a so-called third-party candidate, he received 33 percent of the vote. Abraham Lincoln became the first Republican to win the White House four years later.

162

A brief study of the history of the two parties might reveal surprising information—many of the "historical" positions of the parties seem contradictory to the stands taken by party officials today. The person who reads about political party histories is also likely to conclude that our political parties tend to be driven by differences in ideology more than by personalities, a fact that is blurred today. Third parties have a long-standing tradition in American politics.

Third-Party Politics

Information about today's most popular third-party organizations can be found on the internet:

★ *The Independence Party*, active primarily in Minnesota and led by Governor Jesse Ventura, can be accessed at www.eindependence.org.

★ *The Reform Party*, founded by Ross Perot, can be accessed at www.reformparty.org.

★ *The Libertarian Party* has a web site at www.lp.org.

★ *The Green Party* of the United States, established by Ralph Nader, can be accessed at www.gpus.org.

Local Precinct Politics

Perhaps the most satisfying way of getting involved in a political party is to attend its rallies and meetings. Get to know local candidates and your state and national representatives through local precinct work. Volunteer at election time to make calls, knock on doors, and help post campaign signs. Those most actively involved, of course, are the people most likely to be elected to attend national party conventions.

You can participate as a party member by posting campaign signs in your yard, placing a bumper sticker on your car, or wearing the campaign pin or button of your choice!

46 Visit Washington, D.C.

You make men love their government and their country by giving them the kind of government and the kind of country that inspire respect and love.

—ZECHARIAH CHAFEE JR.

THERE IS NOTHING THAT INSPIRES patriotism as much as a visit to our nation's capital. No wonder the capital is overrun with busloads of school children and tourists—it is truly the showplace of our nation.

Washington, D.C., is a large city with endless options and much more to see than you could possibly take in on one visit. Planning your first trip could be a challenge if you have never been there before or if you are going on your own.

To begin planning your trip consult travel books and ask for recommendations from friends or people you know who have been there. You can also write to the Washington, D.C., Visitors Association or spend some time on the internet looking for sight-seeing possibilities.

The first thing you may want to do is make a priority list of events, sights, outdoor activities, and special activities your children would enjoy. Be sure everyone making the trip has opportunity to have input into the list.

Once a list is compiled, sort out the "must-sees" from the "can waits." Then decide how many of the "must-sees" you can realistically fit into your allotted time.

The Main Attractions

No doubt, a first visit to the nation's capital will include the main attractions: the Capitol building, the White House, and the major monuments and memorials—the Washington Monument and the Jefferson and Lincoln Memorials. Call or write ahead to find out if tours will be available for the Capitol and White House.

If the House or Senate is in session, you can be admitted to the Gallery section with a pass from your congressional representative. To get a pass, write your congressional representative—do this well in advance (six months is customary). Regardless of the ages in your travel group, visiting Congress is an educational experience. When you request a pass, you may want to ask if you can meet personally with your Senator or Congressperson.

A visit to Arlington National Cemetery is one of the most inspiring sights in Washington. More than 200,000 war dead are buried there. Four unidentified bodies from the nation's four wars of the last century are buried at the Tomb of the Unknowns. Changing of the Guard ceremonies are held every half hour through spring and summer hours and every hour in the fall and winter months. The Korean War Veterans Memorial and the Vietnam Veterans Memorial are also easily accessible.

Bring History to Life

To bring history to life, plan a visit to the National Archives where you can view the original documents of our nation's history—a 1297 version of the Magna Carta, the Declaration of Independence, two pages of the Constitution, and the Bill of Rights.

Washington, D.C., is an excellent vacation destination for children. In addition to its more patriotic and historic sights, the city has many child-friendly places worth a visit, such as the National Zoo, the National Aquarium, the Children's Museum, the National Air and Space Museum, and the Bureau of Printing and Engraving.

Nearby Sites

If you have extra time and transportation, take a drive out of Washington to Mount Vernon, the home of George Washington. A visit to Ford's Theatre is another "real life" place of American history.

Don't worry if you can't see everything in one visit—plan a second visit!

VISIT WASHINGTON, D.C.

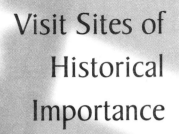

47 Visit Sites of Historical Importance

167

Give me your tired, your poor, your huddled masses yearning to breathe free, the wretched refuse of your teeming shore, Send these, the homeless, tempest-tossed to me; I lift my lamp beside the golden door.

—EMMA LAZARUS

DECIDING TO VISIT OUR NATION'S historic sites in person will take planning. Begin by making a prioritized list of historic U.S. sites that you have not seen and would like to visit.

Take a look at your list when making business travel plans to see if a side trip might be arranged. For cities such as Philadelphia and Washington, D.C., allow several days if possible since there is so much to see.

Keep a journal of what you see and record your feelings and impressions about your tour. Try to imagine the people who made history in each place as being contemporaries rather than historic figures. Encourage children who visit the sites with you to imagine what the historic characters might think of our nation today. Note the differences between cities or buildings at the time of your visit and the time in which various historic events took place. Ask your children to identify the person from history they would most like to meet. What questions might they ask the person?

Virtual Tours

If you cannot visit every place on your list, the worldwide web offers some virtual tours. While virtual tours will not convey the larger-than-life sights, sounds, and smells of historic America, they do provide a sense of what the place is like. Virtual tours are also a great way to prepare for an in-person visit.

For the best virtual tour of our nation's capital, go to http://ahp.gatech.edu/dc_map.html. You can get a sense of the layout of the mall area on the "tourist map." Click on the building you want to see and tour it both inside and out. For more dramatic pictures, go to www.senate.gov/~bennett/photo_tour.html.

If you don't have time to go to Mt. Vernon, you can take a brief tour of George Washington's beautiful home at www.mountvernon.org.

A great place to begin a virtual tour of historic Philadelphia is at http://www.ushistory.org/tour/index.html. You can even participate in a scavenger hunt as you tour the city's historic sites including Independence Hall, the Liberty Bell, and Betsy Ross House to name a few. Go to www.ea.pvt.k12.pa.us/htm/Units/lsDevon/DFormSS/virtualphilly.htm. Each stop includes information about the building, what happened there, and who made it happen.

You can visit historic Colonial Williamsburg at www.aapc.org/conference2000/tour02.htm. A virtual tour available at http://wmbg.com/tour/map_yorktown.html includes the surrounding battlegrounds.

One of the most moving tours of Gettysburg is found at http://www.gettysbg.com/battle.html. Not only will you tour the battleground, but you will learn the facts surrounding this battle.

You can take a virtual tour of Pearl Harbor, with pre- and post-attack pictures at www.hawaii.navy.mil/cnbdata/ cnbdata/7Dec98/virtour.htm.

In Your Area

Do some research about the history of the area where you live. Every state in the nation has a piece of our national history puzzle. Schedule day trips to get a firsthand look at the places that have been important in the development of our nation.

48 Learn about Foreign Lands and Cultures

170

I look upon the whole world as my fatherland. I look upon true patriotism as the brotherhood of man and the service of all to all.

—HELEN KELLER

P ART OF REALLY UNDERSTANDING who we are as Americans involves knowing more about our international origins. Americans come from all over the globe. Archeologists tell us that even Native Americans probably migrated to this continent from another continent. Our diversity is at the root of our determination to preserve the personal freedoms sought by the Pilgrims when they landed at Plymouth Rock, Massachusetts. You can get a sense of how we came to be the nation we are by visiting Ellis Island, New York, in person or on the web at www.ellisisland.com.

Visiting another country can be far more interesting if

you have a personal connection to it—an ancestor, a friend whose family comes from that country, or a business or religious connection. It's best to take your first trip abroad with a tour group or another experienced traveler. That way you can spend your time soaking in the sights, meeting people, and enjoying the uniqueness of your host country rather than fretting about the practical details related to transportation, lodging, and meals.

International travel isn't possible for everyone, however, and there are many other ways to "sample" the cultures that make up our citizenry.

Ethnic Festivals and Events

German Octoberfests as well as Greek festivals, Italian street fairs, and Chinese festivals (just to name a few) are held in cities throughout the United States at various times of the year. These events always welcome the public to sample the food, entertainment, and crafts that are unique to their country of origin. Not only can you and your family sample the culture, but you are also likely to eat some of the most authentic cuisine from the host country. Your local Chamber of Commerce or Tourism Board will be able to tell you when such events are held in your area.

Take an Armchair Tour

Large, glossy books with beautiful photographs are expensive to purchase but free to borrow from the local library. Books designed especially for travelers also provide comprehensive mini-tours and are less expensive than the large photography-oriented books. Check the travel section of your favorite bookstore. *Best bet:* Buy books for countries you actually plan to visit.

Take a Virtual Tour

The worldwide web has connected us with nearly every nation on the planet. You can "travel" to the country of your choice, read its newspapers (in English), watch the current weather there on a live video camera, or connect to sites designed for students and immigrants of that nation who are currently in the United States. Use your favorite search engine to link you with the countries you want to visit. *Hint:* Look for web addresses that end with letters from the name of the country to increase the chances that you are visiting an authentic site.

Here are a few "tours" you can use to get you started:

★ A web site called Virtual World Tour (found at www.chatham-nj.org/coin/sbs/tech/VWT/welcome.htm) offers tours of twenty-one countries. It's a great trip for people of any age although it was originally created with children in mind. Click on a country and away you go! You begin your "trip" in each nation's embassy in Washington, D.C. You can play the national anthem, see the flag, check on today's weather there, view noteworthy sites (click on links that mention tourism) and in some cases, even learn a few phrases from the country's language.

Take time to learn a little about the nation's people, major industries, and political system. Then hurry out to visit cities and people. You might even connect with a new pen pal. You may be able to tour some of the major cities in detail. In Norway, for example, you can slip off to Bergen, the country's second largest city, and stroll through the Bergen Aquarium or tour Troldhaugen, the home of composer Edvard Grieg.

★ You can select from more than a hundred city or country destinations at www.virtualfreesites.com/world.html. This

172

site also has an excellent selection of traveling tips, world maps, world times, travelers warnings, health information, brochures to order, world weather forecasts, world restaurant guides, hostels, and information about specialized travel news groups.

★ Another great place from which to launch a virtual world tour is www.beatricene.com/school/orange_team/sites.html.

★ Explore the medieval castles in Wales at www. castlewales.com/home.html. Visit Irish castles at www.historic. irishcastles.com or www.ireland-now.com/castles/castle1.html.

★ Have you ever wished you could *really* explore the Pyra- mids of Egypt and help solve a mystery or two? You have your chance to do just that at National Geographic's mummy in- vestigation web site: www.nationalgeographic.com/channel/ mummy/. A 3-D tour will let you see the tombs and collect clues from your "dig."

The more you know about world history and the nations of the world, the more insight you will gain into why we Americans are the way we are.

49 Pay Taxes without Complaining

Taxes are what we pay for civilized society.

—OLIVER WENDELL HOLMES JR.

PROBABLY THE MOST FREQUENTLY voiced complaints against the government are related to paying taxes. Taxes are expensive and we don't always agree with how the government spends the money it collects. But taxation is essential to the well-being of society in order for governments at federal, state, and local levels to carry out their responsibilities to the nation's citizens. Therefore, payment of taxes is required by law.

What Your Taxes Buy

Taxes are collected at federal, state, and local levels. Federal taxes are raised to pay for the national defense, social security benefits, the federal court system, medical care for the poor and elderly, the administration of the government, and numerous other national projects and benefits. Included in the expenses paid by state taxes are costs for state roads, highways, state schools, and universities. Taxes collected at the local level support public schools, pay for the building and maintenance of city streets, and provide for community police and fire protection. The government spends tax money to provide thousands of public services that would otherwise not be available to millions of citizens.

A Controversial Issue

Taxes create controversy. Probably the major difference of opinion is in defining the role of government: its involvement in society, its size, and its limits. The size of the government and the amount of services it provides determine how much its citizens have to pay. The more things we want our government to do the more we should expect to pay for those services.

Another controversy surrounding taxes is whether taxpayers are getting their money's worth from government and if the government is making good use of the money it collects. Citizens have the responsibility not only to pay their taxes but also to call the government to greater accountability in the use of taxpayers' money. Nations that are not governed by responsible citizens often end up working for the benefit of its leaders or special interest groups rather than the good of the nation as a whole.

Another reason people often complain about taxes is that they don't think the tax policy is fair or just. They don't think the tax burden is shared equally among all the citizens.

If you disagree with tax policies, voice your opinion. Contact your political representatives, write letters to newspaper editors, participate in an interest group that shares your viewpoint on government, or join forces with others to more effectively make your opinions heard. The citizens of this country are heard, and tax policies can and do change in response to public opinion.

PAY TAXES WITHOUT COMPLAINING

How We Can Help

Unfortunately, many people choose to disobey the tax laws by not filing a tax return, not reporting all their income on their tax returns, or failing to pay the full amount of the taxes they owe. The Internal Revenue Service estimates that in 1992 individual Americans failed to report or pay a whopping $93.2–$95.3 billion. To put that money in perspective, the tax rebate distributed in 2001 totaled $39 billion.

If we were all more honest in reporting our full income, think of the great benefits for our country. Ninety-three billion dollars is a huge amount of money that could help fund schools, roads, national defense, or emergency management. This boost to the budget could be accomplished without raising taxes or writing new tax laws.

While it's unlikely that people consider it "fun" to pay taxes, it is a responsibility of people in a society to help pay for the benefits they enjoy and to help provide for those who are unable to provide for themselves. As comedian Will Rogers once said, "It's a great country, but you can't live in it for nothing."

50 Pray for Our Nation

If my people who are called by my name will humble themselves, and pray and seek my face, and turn from their wicked ways, then I will hear from heaven, and will forgive their sin and heal their land.

—2 CHRONICLES 7:14

VIRTUALLY ALL RELIGIOUS PEOPLE PRAY. Regardless of your political persuasion or religious affiliation, you should feel free to pray for God to bless our nation—to protect, prosper, and bring spiritual renewal to our nation.

Give Thanks

A significant part of prayer is the offering of thanksgiving and praise.

Give thanks for the bountiful blessings bestowed upon our nation now and in the past. Give thanks for our natural resources, our system of democratic government, our fellow citizens who live humble, good, virtuous lives, and for all who have made personal sacrifices for the common good.

Give thanks for our nation's freedom.

Pray for Our Nation

In praying for our nation, include prayers for your neighborhood, city, and state.

Pray for genuine repentance—a turning from crime, sin, evil, terror, and conflict, coupled with a turning toward goodness, brotherly love, and peace.

Pray for peace in the hearts of our citizens and in the hearts of those who lead our nation, so that those who are at peace within might become peacemakers to those who are in conflict. Pray that our nation might live in peace, at home and among all nations.

Pray for justice on behalf of those who are disenfranchised or suffering from any kind of oppression, neglect, or abuse. Pray for all those who work in the judicial system and in our nation's prisons.

Pray for relief for those in our nation who are suffering from sickness, need, sorrow, natural disaster, or acts of terror. Pray for comfort for all who are mourning the loss of loved ones.

Pray for the right and proper use of our natural resources.

Pray for all who serve our cities, states, and nation as elected or appointed government officials. Pray especially for our president, his cabinet members, the leadership of the Senate and House of Representatives, the justices of the Supreme Court, and the judges of appellate and district courts.

Pray specifically for your elected representatives: your member of Congress, senators, governor, state legislator, mayor, and city council member.

Pray for wisdom to be sought and manifested by all in authority, that they may lead us in ways that are truly beneficial to the common good.

Pray for those who are defending our nation at home and abroad, including those who serve our nation as members of police and fire departments.

Pray for the preservation and strengthening of the national values and institutions that support and ensure our "inalienable rights" to life, liberty, and the pursuit of happiness.

Pray for our nation's farms and fisheries, factories and businesses, professional and entrepreneurial enterprises that the harvest from lands and waters and the works of our hands might be prosperous, and that we as a nation might flourish with quality produce, goods, and services. Pray for a generosity of heart that all who prosper might share with those who do not enjoy a fullness of provision.

Pray for the protection of the innocent in our nation, especially our nation's children.

Pray for our nation's families to be strong. Pray that family members might be knit together in faith, virtue, knowledge, patience, and godly behavior.

Pray for Americans who are traveling or working overseas—pray for their protection and that they might exert a positive influence on those with whom they come in contact.

Pray that God will bless America in all ways, at all times.

Amen . . . may it be so.

APPENDIX A

The Declaration of Independence

(Note: Words are spelled and capitalized as they appear in the original document.)

IN CONGRESS, July 4, 1776.

The unanimous Declaration of the thirteen united States of America,

When in the Course of human events, it becomes necessary for one people to dissolve the political bands which have connected them with another, and to assume among the powers of the earth, the separate and equal station to which the Laws of Nature and of Nature's God entitle them, a decent respect to the opinions of mankind requires that they should declare the causes which impel them to the separation.

We hold these truths to be self-evident, that all men are created equal, that they are endowed by their Creator with certain unalienable Rights, that among these are Life, Liberty and the pursuit of Happiness.—That to secure these rights, Governments are instituted among Men, deriving their just powers from the consent of the governed,—That whenever any Form of Government becomes destructive of these ends, it is the Right of the People to alter or to abolish it, and to institute new Government, laying its foundation on such principles and organizing its powers in such form, as to them shall seem most likely to effect their Safety and Happiness. Prudence, indeed, will dictate that Governments long established should not be changed for light and transient causes; and accordingly all experience hath shewn, that mankind are more disposed to suffer, while evils are sufferable, than to right themselves by abolishing the forms to which they are accustomed. But when a long train of abuses and usurpations, pursuing invariably the same Object evinces a design to reduce them under absolute Despotism, it is their right, it is their duty, to throw off such Government, and to provide new Guards for their future security.—Such has been the patient sufferance of these Colonies; and such is now the necessity which constrains them to alter their former Systems of Government. The history of the present King of Great Britain is a history of repeated injuries and usurpations, all having in direct object the establishment of an absolute Tyranny over these States. To prove this, let Facts be submitted to a candid world.

He has refused his Assent to Laws, the most wholesome and necessary for the public good.

He has forbidden his Governors to pass Laws of immediate and pressing importance, unless suspended in their operation till his Assent should be obtained; and when so suspended, he has utterly neglected to attend to them.

He has refused to pass other Laws for the accommodation of large districts of people, unless those people would relinquish the right of Representation in the Legislature, a right inestimable to them and formidable to tyrants only.

He has called together legislative bodies at places unusual, uncomfortable, and distant from the depository of their public Records, for the sole purpose of fatiguing them into compliance with his measures.

He has dissolved Representative Houses repeatedly, for opposing with manly firmness his invasions on the rights of the people.

He has refused for a long time, after such dissolutions, to cause

182

others to be elected; whereby the Legislative powers, incapable of Annihilation, have returned to the People at large for their exercise; the State remaining in the mean time exposed to all the dangers of invasion from without, and convulsions within.

He has endeavoured to prevent the population of these States; for that purpose obstructing the Laws for Naturalization of Foreigners; refusing to pass others to encourage their migrations hither, and raising the conditions of new Appropriations of Lands.

He has obstructed the Administration of Justice, by refusing his Assent to Laws for establishing Judiciary powers.

He has made Judges dependent on his Will alone, for the tenure of their offices, and the amount and payment of their salaries.

He has erected a multitude of New Offices, and sent hither swarms of Officers to harrass our people, and eat out their substance.

He has kept among us, in times of peace, Standing Armies without the Consent of our legislatures.

He has affected to render the Military independent of and superior to the Civil power.

He has combined with others to subject us to a jurisdiction foreign to our constitution, and unacknowledged by our laws; giving his Assent to their Acts of pretended Legislation:

For Quartering large bodies of armed troops among us:

For protecting them, by a mock Trial, from punishment for any Murders which they should commit on the Inhabitants of these States:

For cutting off our Trade with all parts of the world:

For imposing Taxes on us without our Consent:

For depriving us in many cases, of the benefits of Trial by Jury:

For transporting us beyond Seas to be tried for pretended offences:

For abolishing the free System of English Laws in a neighbouring Province, establishing therein an Arbitrary government, and enlarging its Boundaries so as to render it at once an example and fit instrument for introducing the same absolute rule into these Colonies:

For taking away our Charters, abolishing our most valuable Laws, and altering fundamentally the Forms of our Governments:

For suspending our own Legislatures, and declaring themselves invested with power to legislate for us in all cases whatsoever.

He has abdicated Government here, by declaring us out of his Protection and waging War against us.

He has plundered our seas, ravaged our Coasts, burnt our towns, and destroyed the lives of our people.

He is at this time transporting large Armies of foreign Mercenaries to compleat the works of death, desolation and tyranny, already begun with circumstances of Cruelty & perfidy scarcely paralleled in the most barbarous ages, and totally unworthy the Head of a civilized nation.

He has constrained our fellow Citizens taken Captive on the high Seas to bear Arms against their Country, to become the executioners of their friends and Brethren, or to fall themselves by their Hands.

He has excited domestic insurrections amongst us, and has endeavoured to bring on the inhabitants of our frontiers, the merciless Indian Savages, whose known rule of warfare, is an undistinguished destruction of all ages, sexes and conditions.

In every stage of these Oppressions We have Petitioned for Redress in the most humble terms: Our repeated Petitions have been answered only by repeated injury. A Prince whose character is thus marked by every act which may define a Tyrant, is unfit to be the ruler of a free people.

Nor have We been wanting in attentions to our British brethren. We have warned them from time to time of attempts by their legislature to extend an unwarrantable jurisdiction over us. We have reminded them of the circumstances of our emigration and settlement here. We have appealed to their native justice and magnanimity, and we have conjured them by the ties of our common kindred to disavow these usurpations, which, would inevitably interrupt our connections and correspondence. They too have been deaf to the voice of justice and of consanguinity. We must, therefore, acquiesce in the necessity, which denounces our Separation, and hold them, as we hold the rest of mankind, Enemies in War, in Peace Friends.

We, therefore, the Representatives of the united States of America, in General Congress, Assembled, appealing to the Supreme Judge of the world for the rectitude of our intentions, do, in the Name, and by Authority of the good People of these Colonies, solemnly publish and declare, That these United Colonies are, and of Right ought to be Free and Independent States; that they are Absolved from all Allegiance to the British Crown, and that all political connection between them and the State of Great Britain, is and ought to be totally dissolved; and that as Free and Independent States, they have full Power to levy War, conclude Peace, contract Alliances, establish Commerce, and to do all other Acts and Things which Independent States may of right do. And for the support of this Declaration, with a firm reliance on the protection of divine Providence, we mutually pledge to each other our Lives, our Fortunes and our sacred Honor.

APPENDIX B

The Constitution of the United States of America

WE THE PEOPLE OF THE UNITED STATES, in Order to form a more perfect Union, establish Justice, insure domestic Tranquility, provide for the common defence, promote the general Welfare, and secure the Blessings of Liberty to ourselves and our Posterity, do ordain and establish this Constitution for the United States of America.

Article I

Section 1. All legislative Powers herein granted shall be vested in a Congress of the United States, which shall consist of a Senate and House of Representatives.

Section 2. The House of Representatives shall be composed of Members chosen every second Year by the People of the several States, and the Electors in each State shall have the Qualifications requisite for Electors of the most numerous Branch of the State Legislature.

No Person shall be a Representative who shall not have attained to the age of twenty five Years, and been seven Years a Citizen of the United States, and who shall not, when elected, be an Inhabitant of that State in which he shall be chosen.

Representatives and direct Taxes shall be apportioned among the several States which may be included within this Union, according to their respective Numbers, which shall be determined by adding to the whole Number of free Persons, including those bound to Service for a Term of Years, and excluding Indians not taxed, three fifths of all other Persons. The actual Enumeration shall be made within three Years after the first Meeting of the Congress of the United States, and within every subsequent Term of ten Years, in such Manner as they shall by Law direct. The Number of Representatives shall not exceed one for every thirty Thousand, but each State shall have at Least one Representative; and until such enumeration shall be made, the State of New Hampshire shall be entitled to chuse three, Massachusetts eight, Rhode-Island and Providence Plantations one, Connecticut five, New-York six, New Jersey four, Pennsylvania eight, Delaware one, Maryland six, Virginia ten, North Carolina five, South Carolina five, and Georgia three.

When vacancies happen in the Representation from any State, the Executive Authority thereof shall issue Writs of Election to fill such Vacancies.

The House of Representatives shall chuse their Speaker and other Officers; and shall have the sole Power of Impeachment.

Section 3. The Senate of the United States shall be composed of two Senators from each State, chosen by the Legislature thereof, for six Years; and each Senator shall have one Vote.

Immediately after they shall be assembled in Consequence of the first Election, they shall be divided as equally as may be into three Classes. The Seats of the Senators of the first Class shall be vacated at the Expiration of the second Year, of the second Class at the Expiration of the fourth Year, and of the third Class at the Expiration of the sixth Year, so that one third may be chosen every second Year; and if Vacancies happen by Resignation, or otherwise, during the Recess of the Legislature of any State, the Executive thereof may make temporary Appointments until the next Meeting of the Legislature, which shall then fill such Vacancies.

No Person shall be a Senator who shall not have attained to the Age of thirty Years, and been nine Years a Citizen of the United States, and who shall not, when elected, be an Inhabitant of that State for which he shall be chosen.

The Vice President of the United States shall be President of the Senate, but shall have no Vote, unless they be equally divided.

The Senate shall chuse their other Officers, and also a President pro tempore, in the Absence of the Vice President, or when he shall exercise the Office of President of the United States.

The Senate shall have the sole Power to try all Impeachments. When sitting for that Purpose, they shall be on Oath or Affirmation. When the President of the United States is tried, the Chief Justice shall preside: And no Person shall be convicted without the Concurrence of two thirds of the Members present.

Judgment in Cases of Impeachment shall not extend further than to removal from Office, and disqualification to hold and enjoy any Office of Honor, Trust or Profit under the United States: but the Party convicted shall nevertheless be liable and subject to Indictment, Trial, Judgment and Punishment, according to Law.

Section 4. The Times, Places and Manner of holding Elections for Senators and Representatives, shall be prescribed in each State by the Legislature thereof; but the Congress may at any time by Law make or alter such Regulations, except as to the Places of chusing Senators.

The Congress shall assemble at least once in every Year, and such Meeting shall be on the first Monday in December, unless they shall by Law appoint a different Day.

Section 5. Each House shall be the Judge of the Elections, Returns and Qualifications of its own Members, and a Majority of each shall constitute a Quorum to do Business; but a smaller Number may adjourn from day to day, and may be authorized to compel the Attendance of absent Members, in such Manner, and under such Penalties as each House may provide.

Each House may determine the Rules of its Proceedings, punish its Members for disorderly Behaviour, and, with the Concurrence of two thirds, expel a Member.

Each House shall keep a Journal of its Proceedings, and from time to time publish the same, excepting such Parts as may in their Judgment require Secrecy; and the Yeas and Nays of the Members of either House on any question shall, at the Desire of one fifth of those Present, be entered on the Journal.

Neither House, during the Session of Congress, shall, without the Consent of the other, adjourn for more than three days, nor to any other Place than that in which the two Houses shall be sitting.

189

Section 6. The Senators and Representatives shall receive a Compensation for their Services, to be ascertained by Law, and paid out of the Treasury of the United States. They shall in all Cases, except Treason, Felony and Breach of the Peace, be privileged from Arrest during their Attendance at the Session of their respective Houses, and in going to and returning from the same; and for any Speech or Debate in either House, they shall not be questioned in any other Place.

No Senator or Representative shall, during the Time for which he was elected, be appointed to any civil Office under the Authority of the United States, which shall have been created, or the Emoluments whereof shall have been encreased during such time; and no Person holding any Office under the United States, shall be a Member of either House during his Continuance in Office.

Section 7. All Bills for raising Revenue shall originate in the House of Representatives; but the Senate may propose or concur with Amendments as on other Bills.

Every Bill which shall have passed the House of Representatives and the Senate, shall, before it become a Law, be presented to the President of the United States; If he approve he shall sign it, but if not he shall return it, with his Objections to that House in which it shall have originated, who shall enter the Objections at large on their Journal, and proceed to reconsider it. If after such Reconsideration two thirds of that House shall agree to pass the Bill, it shall be sent, together with the Objections, to the other House, by which it shall likewise be reconsidered, and if approved by two thirds of that House, it shall become a Law. But in all such Cases the Votes of both Houses shall be determined by Yeas and Nays, and the Names of the Persons voting for and against the Bill shall be entered on the Journal of each House respectively. If any Bill shall not be returned by the President within ten Days (Sundays excepted) after it shall have been presented to him, the Same shall be a Law, in like Manner as if he had signed it, unless the Congress by their Adjournment prevent its Return, in which Case it shall not be a Law.

Every Order, Resolution, or Vote to which the Concurrence of the Senate and House of Representatives may be necessary (except on a question of Adjournment) shall be presented to the President of the United States; and before the Same shall take Effect, shall be approved by him, or being disapproved by him, shall be repassed by two thirds of the Senate and House of Representatives, according to the Rules and Limitations prescribed in the Case of a Bill.

Section 8. The Congress shall have Power To lay and collect Taxes, Duties, Imposts and Excises, to pay the Debts and provide for the common Defence and general Welfare of the United States; but all Duties, Imposts and Excises shall be uniform throughout the United States;

To borrow Money on the credit of the United States;

To regulate Commerce with foreign Nations, and among the several States, and with the Indian Tribes;

To establish an uniform Rule of Naturalization, and uniform Laws on the subject of Bankruptcies throughout the United States;

To coin Money, regulate the Value thereof, and of foreign Coin, and fix the Standard of Weights and Measures;

To provide for the Punishment of counterfeiting the Securities and current Coin of the United States;

To establish Post Offices and post Roads;

To promote the Progress of Science and useful Arts, by securing for limited Times to Authors and Inventors the exclusive Right to their respective Writings and Discoveries;

To constitute Tribunals inferior to the supreme Court;

To define and punish Piracies and Felonies committed on the high Seas, and Offenses against the Law of Nations;

To declare War, grant Letters of Marque and Reprisal, and make Rules concerning Captures on Land and Water;

To raise and support Armies, but no Appropriation of Money to that Use shall be for a longer Term than two Years;

To provide and maintain a Navy;

To make Rules for the Government and Regulation of the land and naval Forces;

To provide for calling forth the Militia to execute the Laws of the Union, suppress Insurrections and repel Invasions;

To provide for organizing, arming, and disciplining, the Militia, and for governing such Part of them as may be employed in the Service of the United States, reserving to the States respectively, the Appointment of the Officers, and the Authority of training the Militia according to the discipline prescribed by Congress;

To exercise exclusive Legislation in all Cases whatsoever, over such District (not exceeding ten Miles square) as may, by Cession of particular States, and the Acceptance of Congress, become the Seat of the Government of the United States, and to exercise like Authority over all Places purchased by the Consent of the Legislature of the State in which the Same shall be, for the Erection of Forts, Magazines, Arsenals, dock-Yards, and other needful Buildings—And

To make all Laws which shall be necessary and proper for carrying into Execution the foregoing Powers, and all other Powers vested by this Constitution in the Government of the United States, or in any Department or Officer thereof.

Section 9. The Migration or Importation of such Persons as any of the States now existing shall think proper to admit, shall not be prohibited by the Congress prior to the Year one thousand eight hundred and eight, but a Tax or duty may be imposed on such Importation, not exceeding ten dollars for each Person.

The Privilege of the Writ of Habeas Corpus shall not be suspended, unless when in Cases of Rebellion or Invasion the public Safety may require it.

No Bill of Attainder or ex post facto Law shall be passed.

No Capitation, or other direct, Tax shall be laid, unless in Proportion to the Census or Enumeration herein before directed to be taken.

No Tax or Duty shall be laid on Articles exported from any State.

No Preference shall be given by any Regulation of Commerce or Revenue to the Ports of one State over those of another: nor shall Vessels bound to, or from, one State, be obliged to enter, clear, or pay Duties in another.

No Money shall be drawn from the Treasury, but in Consequence of Appropriations made by Law; and a regular Statement and Account of the Receipts and Expenditures of all public Money shall be published from time to time.

No Title of Nobility shall be granted by the United States: And no Person holding any Office of Profit or Trust under them, shall, without the Consent of the Congress, accept of any present, Emolument, Office, or Title, of any kind whatever, from any King, Prince, or foreign State.

Section 10. No State shall enter into any Treaty, Alliance, or Confederation; grant Letters of Marque and Reprisal; coin Money; emit Bills of Credit; make any Thing but gold and silver Coin a Tender in Payment of Debts; pass any Bill of Attainder, ex post facto Law, or Law impairing the Obligation of Contracts, or grant any Title of Nobility.

No State shall, without the Consent of the Congress, lay any Imposts or Duties on Imports or Exports, except what may be absolutely necessary for executing it's inspection Laws: and the net Produce of all Duties and Imposts, laid by any State on Imports or Exports, shall be for the Use of the Treasury of the United States; and all such Laws shall be subject to the Revision and Controul of the Congress.

No State shall, without the Consent of Congress, lay any Duty of Tonnage, keep Troops, or Ships of War in time of Peace, enter into any Agreement or Compact with another State, or with a foreign Power, or engage in War, unless actually invaded, or in such imminent Danger as will not admit of delay.

Article II

Section 1. The executive Power shall be vested in a President of the United States of America. He shall hold his Office during the Term of four Years, and, together with the Vice President, chosen for the same Term, be elected, as follows:

Each State shall appoint, in such Manner as the Legislature thereof may direct, a Number of Electors, equal to the whole Number of Senators and Representatives to which the State may be entitled in the Congress: but no Senator or Representative, or Person holding an Office of Trust or Profit under the United States, shall be appointed an Elector.

The Electors shall meet in their respective States, and vote by Ballot for two Persons, of whom one at least shall not be an Inhabitant of the same State with themselves. And they shall make a List of all the Persons voted for, and of the Number of Votes for each; which List they shall sign and certify, and transmit sealed to the Seat of the Government of the United States, directed to the President of the Senate. The President of the Senate shall, in the Presence of the Senate and House of Representatives, open all the Certificates, and the Votes shall then be counted. The Person having the greatest Number of Votes shall be the President, if such Number be a Majority of the whole Number of Electors appointed; and if there be more than one who have such Majority, and have an equal Number of Votes, then the House of Representatives shall immediately chuse by Ballot one of them for President; and if no Person have a Majority, then from the five highest on the List the said House shall in like Manner chuse the President. But in chusing the President, the Votes shall be taken by States, the Representation from each State having one Vote; A quorum for this Purpose shall consist of a Member or Members from two thirds of the States, and a Majority of all the States shall be necessary to a Choice. In every Case, after the Choice of the President, the Person having the greatest Number of Votes of the Electors shall be the Vice President. But if there should remain two or more who have equal Votes, the Senate shall chuse from them by Ballot the Vice President.

The Congress may determine the Time of chusing the Electors, and the Day on which they shall give their Votes; which Day shall be the same throughout the United States.

No Persons except a natural born Citizen, or a Citizen of the United States, at the time of the Adoption of this Constitution, shall be eligible to the Office of President; neither shall any Person be eligible to that Office who shall not have attained to the Age of thirty five Years, and been fourteen Years a Resident within the United States.

In Case of the Removal of the President from Office, or of his Death, Resignation, or Inability to discharge the Powers and Duties of the said Office, the Same shall devolve on the Vice President, and the Congress may by Law provide for the Case of Removal, Death, Resignation or Inability, both of the President and Vice President, declaring what Officer shall then act as President, and such Officer shall act accordingly, until the Disability be removed, or a President shall be elected.

The President shall, at stated Times, receive for his Services, a Compensation, which shall neither be increased nor diminished during the Period for which he shall have been elected, and he shall not receive within that Period any other Emolument from the United States, or any of them.

Before he enter on the Execution of his Office, he shall take the following Oath or Affirmation:—"I do solemnly swear (or affirm) that I will faithfully execute the Office of President of the United States, and will to the best of my Ability, preserve, protect and defend the Constitution of the United States."

Section 2. The President shall be Commander in Chief of the Army and Navy of the United States, and of the Militia of the several States, when called into the actual Service of the United States; he may require the Opinion, in writing, of the principal Officer in each of the executive Departments, upon any Subject relating to the Duties of their respective Offices, and he shall have Power to grant Reprieves and Pardons for Offenses against the United States, except in Cases of Impeachment.

He shall have Power, by and with the Advice and Consent of the Senate, to make Treaties, provided two thirds of the Senators present concur; and he shall nominate, and by and with the Advice and Consent of the Senate, shall appoint Ambassadors, other public Ministers and Consuls, Judges of the supreme Court, and all other Officers of the United States, whose Appointments are not herein otherwise provided for, and which shall be established by Law: but the Congress may by Law vest the Appointment of such inferior Officers, as they think proper, in the President alone, in the Courts of Law, or in the Heads of Departments.

The President shall have Power to fill up all Vacancies that may happen during the Recess of the Senate, by granting Commissions which shall expire at the End of their next Session.

Section 3. He shall from time to time give to the Congress Information of the State of the Union, and recommend to their Consideration such Measures as he shall judge necessary and expedient; he may, on extraordinary Occasions, convene both Houses, or either of them, and in Case of Disagreement between them, with Respect to the Time of Adjournment, he may adjourn them to such Time as he shall think proper; he shall receive Ambassadors and other public Ministers; he shall take Care that the Laws be faithfully executed, and shall Commission all the Officers of the United States.

Section 4. The President, Vice President and all civil Officers of the United States, shall be removed from Office on Impeachment for, and Conviction of, Treason, Bribery, or other high Crimes and Misdemeanors.

Article III

Section 1. The judicial Power of the United States, shall be vested in one supreme Court, and in such inferior Courts as the Congress may from time to time ordain and establish. The Judges, both of the supreme and inferior Courts, shall hold their Offices during good Behaviour, and shall, at stated Times, receive for their Services, a Compensation, which shall not be diminished during their Continuance in Office.

Section 2. The judicial Power shall extend to all Cases, in Law and Equity, arising under this Constitution, the Laws of the United States, and Treaties made, or which shall be made, under their Authority;

to all Cases affecting Ambassadors, other public Ministers and Consuls;—to all Cases of admiralty and maritime Jurisdiction;—to Controversies to which the United States shall be a Party:—to Controversies between two or more States;—between a State and Citizens of another State;—between Citizens of different States;—between Citizens of the same State claiming Lands under Grants of different States, and between a State, or the Citizens thereof, and foreign States, Citizens or Subjects.

In all Cases affecting Ambassadors, other public Ministers and Consuls, and those in which a State shall be Party, the supreme Court shall have original Jurisdiction. In all the other Cases before mentioned, the supreme Court shall have appellate Jurisdiction, both as to Law and Fact, with such Exceptions, and under such Regulations as the Congress shall make.

The Trial of all Crimes, except in Cases of Impeachment, shall be by Jury; and such Trial shall be held in the State where the said Crimes shall have been committed; but when not committed within any State, the Trial shall be at such Place or Places as the Congress may by Law have directed.

Section 3. Treason against the United States, shall consist only in levying War against them, or in adhering to their Enemies, giving them Aid and Comfort. No Person shall be convicted of Treason unless on the Testimony of two Witnesses to the same overt Act, or on Confession in open Court.

The Congress shall have Power to declare the Punishment of Treason, but no Attainder of Treason shall work Corruption of Blood, or Forfeiture except during the Life of the Person attained.

Article IV

Section 1. Full Faith and Credit shall be given in each State to the public Acts, Records, and judicial Proceedings of every other State. And the Congress may by general Laws prescribe the Manner in which such Acts, Records, and Proceedings shall be proved, and the Effect thereof.

Section 2. The Citizens of each State shall be entitled to all Privileges and Immunities of Citizens in the several States.

A Person charged in any State with Treason, Felony, or other Crime, who shall flee from Justice, and be found in another State, shall on Demand of the executive Authority of the State from which he fled, be delivered up, to be removed to the State having Jurisdiction of the Crime.

No Person held to Service or Labour in one State, under the Laws thereof, escaping into another, shall, in Consequence of any Law or Regulation therein, be discharged from such Service or Labour, but shall be delivered up on Claim of the Party to whom such Service or Labour may be due.

Section 3. New States may be admitted by the Congress into this Union; but no new State shall be formed or erected within the Jurisdiction of any other State; nor any State be formed by the Junction of two or more States, or Parts of States, without the Consent of the Legislatures of the States concerned as well as of the Congress.

The Congress shall have Power to dispose of and make all needful Rules and Regulations respecting the Territory or other Property belonging to the United States; and nothing in this Constitution shall be so construed as to Prejudice any Claims of the United States, or of any particular State.

Section 4. The United States shall guarantee to every State in this Union a Republican Form of Government, and shall protect each of them against Invasion; and on Application of the Legislature, or of the Executive (when the Legislature cannot be convened) against domestic Violence.

Article V

The Congress, whenever two thirds of both Houses shall deem it necessary, shall propose Amendments to this Constitution, or, on the Application of the Legislatures of two thirds of the several States, shall call a Convention for proposing Amendments, which, in either Case, shall be valid to all Intents and Purposes, as Part of this Constitution, when ratified by the Legislatures of three fourths of the several States, or by Conventions in three fourths thereof, as the one or the other Mode of Ratification may be proposed by the Congress; Provided that no Amendment which may be made prior to the Year One thousand eight hundred and eight shall in any Manner affect the first and fourth Clauses in the Ninth Section of the first Article; and that no State, without its Consent, shall be deprived of its equal Suffrage in the Senate.

Article VI

All Debts contracted and Engagements entered into, before the Adoption of this Constitution, shall be as valid against the United States under this Constitution, as under the Confederation.

This Constitution, and the Laws of the United States which shall be made in Pursuance thereof; and all Treaties made, or which shall be made, under the Authority of the United States, shall be the supreme Law of the Land; and the Judges in every State shall be bound thereby, any Thing in the Constitution or Laws of any State to the Contrary notwithstanding.

The Senators and Representatives before mentioned, and the Members of the several State Legislatures, and all executive and judicial Officers, both of the United States and of the several States, shall be bound by Oath or Affirmation, to support this Constitution; but no religious Test shall ever be required as a Qualification to any Office or public Trust under the United States.

Article VII

The Ratification of the Conventions of nine States, shall be sufficient for the Establishment of this Constitution between the States so ratifying the Same.

Done in Convention by the Unanimous Consent of the States present the Seventeenth Day of September in the Year of our Lord one thousand seven hundred and Eighty seven and of the Independence of the United States of America the Twelfth. In Witness whereof We have hereunto subscribed our Names,

196

—*George Washington*—President and deputy from Virginia

APPENDIX C

The Bill of Rights

(Note: The following text is a transcription of the first ten amendments to the Constitution in their original form. The spelling has been corrected to comply with current usage.)

Amendment I

Congress shall make no law respecting an establishment of religion, or prohibiting the free exercise thereof; or abridging the freedom of speech, or of the press; or the right of the people peaceably to assemble, and to petition the Government for a redress of grievances.

Amendment II

A well regulated Militia, being necessary to the security of a free State, the right of the people to keep and bear Arms, shall not be infringed.

Amendment III

No Soldier shall, in time of peace be quartered in any house, without the consent of the Owner, nor in time of war, but in a manner to be prescribed by law.

Amendment IV

The right of the people to be secure in their persons, houses, papers, and effects, against unreasonable searches and seizures, shall not be violated, and no Warrants shall issue, but upon probable cause, supported by Oath or affirmation, and particularly describing the place to be searched, and the persons or things to be seized.

Amendment V

No person shall be held to answer for a capital, or otherwise infamous crime, unless on a presentment or indictment of a Grand Jury, except in cases arising in the land or naval forces, or in the Militia, when in actual service in time of War or public danger; nor shall any person be subject for the same offence to be twice put in jeopardy of life or limb, nor shall be compelled in any criminal case to be a witness against himself, nor be deprived of life, liberty, or property, without due process of law; nor shall private property be taken for public use, without just compensation.

Amendment VI

In all criminal prosecutions, the accused shall enjoy the right to a speedy and public trial, by an impartial jury of the State and district wherein the crime shall have been committed, which district shall have been previously ascertained by law, and to be informed of the nature and cause of the accusation; to be confronted with the witnesses against him; to have compulsory process for obtaining witnesses in his favor, and to have the assistance of counsel for his defence.

Amendment VII

In Suits at common law, where the value in controversy shall exceed twenty dollars, the right of trial by jury shall be preserved, and no fact tried by a jury, shall be otherwise reexamined in any Court of the United States, than according to the rules of the common law.

Amendment VIII

Excessive bail shall not be required, nor excessive fines imposed, nor cruel and unusual punishments inflicted.

Amendment IX

The enumeration in the Constitution, of certain rights, shall not be construed to deny or disparage others retained by the people.

Amendment X

The powers not delegated to the United States by the Constitution, nor prohibited by it to the States, are reserved to the States respectively, or to the people.

APPENDIX D

Lyrics to Patriotic Songs

America the Beautiful

By Katharine Lee Bates

O beautiful for spacious skies,
For amber waves of grain,
For purple mountain majesties
Above the fruited plain!
America! America!
God shed his grace on thee
And crown thy good with brotherhood
From sea to shining sea!

O beautiful for pilgrim feet
Whose stern, impassioned stress
A thoroughfare for freedom beat
Across the wilderness!
America! America!
God mend thine every flaw,
Confirm thy soul in self-control,
Thy liberty in law!

O beautiful for heroes proved,
In liberating strife,
Who more than self their country loved
And mercy more than life!
America! America!
May God thy gold refine
Till all success be nobleness
And every gain divine!

O beautiful for patriot dream
That sees beyond the years
Thine alabaster cities gleam
Undimmed by human tears!
America! America!
God shed his grace on thee
And crown thy good with brotherhood
From sea to shining sea!

200

O beautiful for halcyon skies,
For amber waves of grain,
For purple mountain majesties
Above the enameled plain!
America! America!
God shed his grace on thee
Till souls wax fair as earth and air
And music-hearted sea!

O beautiful for pilgrim feet,
Whose stern impassioned stress
A thoroughfare for freedom beat
Across the wilderness!
America! America!
God shed his grace on thee
Till paths be wrought through
wilds of thought

By pilgrim foot and knee!
O beautiful for glory-tale
Of liberating strife
When once and twice,
for man's avail
Men lavished precious life !
America! America!
God shed his grace on thee
Till selfish gain no longer stain
The banner of the free!

201

O beautiful for patriot dream
That sees beyond the years
Thine alabaster cities gleam
Undimmed by human tears!
America! America!
God shed his grace on thee
Till nobler men keep once again
Thy whiter jubilee!

The Star-Spangled Banner

By Francis Scott Key, 1814

O say, can you see, by the dawn's early light,
What so proudly we hail'd at the twilight's last gleaming?
Whose broad stripes and bright stars, thro' the perilous fight,
O'er the ramparts we watch'd, were so gallantly streaming?
And the rockets' red glare, the bombs bursting in air,
Gave proof thro' the night that our flag was still there.
O say, does that star-spangled banner yet wave
O'er the land of the free and the home of the brave?

On the shore dimly seen thro' the mists of the deep,
Where the foe's haughty host in dread silence reposes,
What is that which the breeze, o'er the towering steep,
As it fitfully blows, half conceals, half discloses?
Now it catches the gleam of the morning's first beam,
In full glory reflected, now shines on the stream:
'Tis the star-spangled banner: O, long may it wave
O'er the land of the free and the home of the brave!

And where is that band who so vauntingly swore
That the havoc of war and the battle's confusion,
A home and a country should leave us no more?
Their blood has wash'd out their foul footsteps' pollution.
No refuge could save the hireling and slave
From the terror of flight or the gloom of the grave:
And the star-spangled banner in triumph doth wave
O'er the land of the free and the home of the brave.

O thus be it ever when free-men shall stand
Between their lov'd home and the war's desolation;
Blest with vict'ry and peace, may the heav'n-rescued land
Praise the Pow'r that hath made and preserv'd us a nation!
Then conquer we must, when our cause it is just,
And this be our motto: "In God is our trust!"
And the star-spangled banner in triumph shall wave
O'er the land of the free and the home of the brave!

You're a Grand Old Flag

You're a Grand Old Flag
You're a High Flying Flag
And forever, in peace, may you wave!
You're the emblem of the land I love,
The home of the free and the brave!

202

Ev'ry heart beats true 'neath the Red, White, and Blue,
Where there's never a boast or brag.
But should auld acquaintance be forgot
Keep your eye on the Grand Old Flag!
I'm a cranky hanky panky,
I'm a dead square, honest Yankee,
And I'm mighty proud of that old flag
That flies for Uncle Sam.
Though I don't believe in raving
Ev'ry time I see it waving,
There's a chill runs up my back that makes me glad I'm what I am.   203

Here's a land with a million soldiers,
That's if we should need 'em,
We'll fight for freedom!
Hurrah! Hurrah! For every Yankee tar
And old G.A.R.
Ev'ry stripe, ev'ry star.
Red, white and blue,
Hats off to you
Honest, you're a grand old flag!

You're a Grand Old Flag
You're a High Flying Flag
And forever, in peace, may you wave!
You're the emblem of the land I love,
The home of the free and the brave!
Ev'ry heart beats true 'neath the Red, White, and Blue,
Where there's never a boast or brag.
But should auld acquaintance be forgot
Keep your eye on the Grand Old Flag!

My Country, 'tis of Thee

By Samuel Francis Smith

My country, 'tis of thee,
Sweet land of Liberty,
Of thee I sing;
Land where my fathers died,
Land of the pilgrim's pride!
From ev'ry mountain side,
Let freedom ring!

My native country thee,
Land of the noble free,
Thy name I love.
I love thy rocks and rills,
Thy woods and templed hills;
My heart with rapture thrills,
Like that above.

Let music swell the breeze,
And ring from all the trees,
Sweet freedom's song.
Let mortal tongues awake;
Let all that breathe partake;
Let rocks their silence break,
the sound prolong.

Our fathers' God, to Thee,
Author of Liberty,
To Thee we sing.
Long may our land be bright,
With freedom's holy light;
Protect us by Thy might,
Great God, our King!

APPENDIX E

Gettysburg Address

Abraham Lincoln
NOVEMBER 19, 1863

Four score and seven years ago our fathers brought forth on this continent, a new nation, conceived in Liberty, and dedicated to the proposition that all men are created equal.

Now we are engaged in a great civil war, testing whether that nation, or any nation so conceived and so dedicated, can long endure. We are met on a great battle-field of that war. We have come to dedicate a portion of that field, as a final resting place for those who here gave their lives that that nation might live. It is altogether fitting and proper that we should do this.

But, in a larger sense, we can not dedicate—we can not consecrate—we can not hallow—this ground. The brave men, living and dead, who struggled here, have consecrated it, far above our poor power to add or detract. The world will little note, nor long remember what we say here, but it can never forget what they did here. It is for us the living, rather, to be dedicated here to the unfinished work which they who fought here have thus far so nobly advanced. It is rather for us to be here dedicated to the great task remaining before us—that from these honored dead we take increased devotion to that cause for which they gave the last full measure of devotion—that we here highly resolve that these dead shall not have died in vain—that this nation, under God, shall have a new birth of freedom—and that government of the people, by the people, for the people, shall not perish from the earth.

206

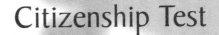

APPENDIX F

Citizenship Test

(Reprinted from the Department of Justice, Immigration & Naturalization Service web site.)

One Hundred Typical Questions

1. What are the colors of our flag?
2. How many stars are there in our flag?
3. What color are the stars on our flag?
4. What do the stars on the flag mean?
5. How many stripes are there in the flag?
6. What color are the stripes?
7. What do the stripes on the flag mean?
8. How many states are there in the union?
9. What is the 4th of July?
10. What is the date of Independence Day?
11. Independence from whom?
12. What country did we fight during the Revolutionary War?
13. Who was the first president of the United States?
14. Who is the president of the United States today?
15. Who is the vice president of the United States today?
16. Who elects the president of the United States?
17. Who becomes president of the United States if the president should die?
18. For how long do we elect the president?
19. What is the Constitution?

20. Can the Constitution be changed?
21. What do we call a change to the Constitution?
22. How many changes or amendments are there to the Constitution?
23. How many branches are there in our government?
24. What are the three branches of our government?
25. What is the legislative branch of our government?
26. Who makes the laws in the United States?
27. What is Congress?
28. What are the duties of Congress?
29. Who elects Congress?
30. How many senators are there in Congress?
31. Can you name the two senators from your state?
32. For how long do we elect each senator?
33. How many representatives are there in Congress?
34. For how long do we elect the representatives?
35. What is the executive branch of our government?
36. What is the judiciary branch of our government?
37. What are the duties of the Supreme Court?
38. What is the supreme law of the United States?
39. What is the Bill of Rights?
40. What is the capital of your state?
41. Who is the current governor of your state?
42. Who becomes president of the United States of America if the president and the vice president should die?
43. Who is the chief justice of the Supreme Court?
44. Can you name the thirteen original states?
45. Who said, "Give me liberty or give me death"?
46. Which countries were our enemies during World War II?
47. What are the 49th and 50th states of the union?
48. How many terms can a president serve?
49. Who was Martin Luther King Jr.?
50. Who is the head of your local government?
51. According to the Constitution, a person must meet certain

requirements in order to be eligible to become president. Name one of these requirements.

52. Why are there one hundred senators in the Senate?
53. Who selects the Supreme Court justices?
54. How many Supreme Court justices are there?
55. Why did the Pilgrims come to America?
56. What is the head executive of a state government called?
57. What is the head executive of a city government called?
58. What holiday was celebrated for the first time by the American colonists?
59. Who was the main writer of the Declaration of Independence?
60. When was the Declaration of Independence adopted?
61. What is the basic belief of the Declaration of Independence?
62. What is the national anthem of the United States?
63. Who wrote the "Star-Spangled Banner"?
64. Where does freedom of speech come from?
65. What is the minimum voting age in the United States?
66. Who signs bills into law?
67. What is the highest court in the United States?
68. Who was the president during the Civil War?
69. What did the Emancipation Proclamation do?
70. What special group advises the president?
71. Which president is called the "Father of our country"?
72. What immigration and naturalization service form is used to apply to become a naturalized citizen?
73. Who helped the Pilgrims in America?
74. What is the name of the ship that brought the Pilgrims to America?
75. What were the 13 original states of the United States called?
76. Name 3 rights or freedoms guaranteed by the Bill of Rights.

77. Who has the power to declare war?
78. What kind of government does the United States have?
79. Which president freed the slaves?
80. In what year was the Constitution written?
81. What are the first 10 amendments to the Constitution called?
82. Name one purpose of the United Nations.
83. Where does Congress meet?
84. Whose rights are guaranteed by the Constitution and the Bill of Rights?
85. What is the introduction to the Constitution called?
86. Name one benefit of being a citizen of the United States.
87. What is the most important right granted to United States citizens?
88. What is the United States Capitol?
89. What is the White House?
90. Where is the White House located?
91. What is the name of the president's official home?
92. Name one right guaranteed by the First Amendment.
93. Who is the commander in chief of the United States military?
94. Which president was the first commander in chief of the United States military?
95. In what month do we vote for the president?
96. In what month is the new president inaugurated?
97. How many times may a senator be reelected?
98. How many times may a congressman be reelected?
99. What are the 2 major political parties in the United States today?
100. How many states are there in the United States?

Answers

1. Red, white, and blue
2. 50
3. White
4. One for each state in the Union
5. 13
6. Red and white
7. They represent the original 13 states
8. 50
9. Independence Day
10. July 4th
11. England
12. England
13. George Washington
14. George W. Bush
15. Dick Cheney
16. The Electoral College
17. Vice President
18. Four years
19. The supreme law of the land
20. Yes
21. Amendments
22. 27
23. 3
24. Legislative, executive, and judicial
25. Congress
26. Congress
27. The Senate and the House of Representatives

28. To make laws
29. The people
30. 100
31. (Insert local information)
32. 6 years
33. 435
34. 2 years
35. The president, cabinet, and departments under the cabinet members
36. The Supreme Court
37. To interpret laws
38. The Constitution
39. The first 10 amendments of the Constitution
40. (Insert local information)
41. (Insert local information)
42. Speaker of the House of Representatives
43. William Rehnquist
44. Connecticut, New Hampshire, New York, New Jersey, Massachusetts, Pennsylvania, Delaware, Virginia, North Carolina, South Carolina, Georgia,

211

Rhode Island, and
Maryland
45. Patrick Henry
46. Germany, Italy, and
Japan
47. Hawaii and Alaska
48. 2
49. A civil rights leader
50. (Insert local
information)

51. Must be a natural born
citizen of the United
States; must be at least 35
years old by the time he/
she will serve; must have
lived in the United States
for at least 14 years
52. Two (2) from each state
53. Appointed by the
president
54. 9
55. For religious freedom
56. Governor
57. Mayor
58. Thanksgiving
59. Thomas Jefferson
60. July 4, 1776
61. That all men are created
equal
62. "The Star-Spangled
Banner"
63. Francis Scott Key
64. The Bill of Rights
65. 18
66. The president

67. The Supreme Court
68. Abraham Lincoln
69. Freed many slaves
70. The cabinet
71. George Washington
72. Form N-400,
"Application to File
Petition for
Naturalization"
73. The American Indians
(Native Americans)
74. The *Mayflower*
75. Colonies
76. (A) The rights of
freedom of speech, press,
religion, peaceable
assembly, and requesting
change of government.
(B) The right to bear
arms (the right to have
weapons or own a gun,
though subjected to
certain regulations).
(C) The government
may not quarter, or
house, soldiers in the
people's homes during
peacetime without the
people's consent.
(D) The government
may not search or take a
person's property
without a warrant.
(E) A person may not be
tried twice for the same

crime and does not have to testify against himself.

(F) A person charged with a crime still has some rights, such as the right to a trial and to have a lawyer.

(G) The right to trial by jury in most cases.

(H) Protects people against excessive or unreasonable fines or cruel and unusual punishment.

(L) The people have rights other than those mentioned in the Constitution, any power not given to the federal government by the Constitution is a power of either the state or the people

77. Congress
78. Republican
79. Abraham Lincoln
80. 1787
81. The Bill of Rights
82. For countries to discuss and try to resolve world problems; to provide economic aid to many countries
83. In the Capitol in Washington, D.C.

84. Everyone (citizens and noncitizens living in the United States)
85. The Preamble
86. Obtain federal government jobs; travel with a United States passport; petition for close relatives to come to the United States to live
87. The right to vote
88. The place where Congress meets
89. The president's official home
90. Washington, D.C. (1600 Pennsylvania Avenue, NW)
91. The White House
92. Freedom of speech, press, religion, peaceable assembly, and requesting change of the government
93. The President
94. George Washington
95. November
96. January
97. There is no limit
98. There is no limit
99. Democratic and Republican
100. 50

Popular Books by Starburst Publishers®

Fifty Ways to Stand Up for America
By W. B. Freeman

Rev up your patriotic spirit with heart-warming anecdotes, how-to advice, interesting historical information, and practical tips. Learn flag flying etiquette. Discover the benefits and responsibilities of good citizenship. Be inspired to take part in your community, and find that one-for-all-and-all-for-one attitude.

(trade paper)   ISBN 1892016702   **$11.99**

Cheap Talk with the Frugal Friends
By Angie Zalewski and Deana Ricks

A collection of savvy tips and tricks for stretching the family dollar from the celebrity thrifters known as the Frugal Friends by their radio and television audiences. This book is packed with money-saving tips on various topics including automotive, beauty care, cleaning, dating, decorating, medicine, pet care, and sporting goods.

(trade paper)   ISBN 1892016583   **$9.99**

Incredible KidEdibles
By Beth Brigham

Discover over 125 recipes for easy-to-make critters, airplanes, and boats. Make unforgettable party snacks, tasty art projects, memorable holiday snacks, and edible doughs. Each snack is illustrated to help you craft magic for and with kids. Create a snack and a smile.

(trade paper)   ISBN 1892016451   **$12.99**

Stories for the Spirit-Filled™ Believer
Edited by Cristine Bolley

It's one thing to know that God is real. It is quite another to have profound and ongoing experiences that confirm that belief. This volume includes stories from Oral Roberts, Jesse Duplantis, T. D. Jakes, Joyce Meyer, and more. Each selection contains a Scripture verse, true story, and a prayer. Sure to inspire readers to listen for God's voice in their own lives.

(trade paper)   ISBN 1892016540   **$13.99**

The Bible—God's Word for the Biblically-Inept™
By Larry Richards

An excellent book to start learning the entire Bible. Get the basics or the in-depth information you seek with this user-friendly overview. From Creation to Christ to the Millennium, learning the Bible has never been easier. The best-selling *God's Word for the Biblically-Inept*™ series mixes scholarly information from experts with helpful icons, illustrations, sidebars, and timelines.

(trade paper)   ISBN 0914984551   **$16.95**

Revelation—God's Word for the Biblically-Inept™
By Daymond R. Duck

End-time Bible prophecy expert Daymond R. Duck leads readers verse by verse through one of the Bible's most confusing books. Follow the experts as they explain the captivating prophecies of Revelation and point out related current events! Over 100,000 sold!

(trade paper)   ISBN 0914984985   **$16.95**

The Bible for Teens: Learn the Word™

In a special adaptation just for teens, the unique Biblically-Inept™ brand of simplified Bible commentary is blended with content and features aimed directly at today's youth. Popular elements from the original series such as chapter summaries, definitions, timelines, illustrations, and study questions are combined with new features including "Your Move" and "Get Real." Finally, a complete overview of the entire Bible—from Creation to Christ to Armageddon and beyond—just for teens.

(trade paper)   ISBN 1892016516   **$14.99**

Revelation for Teens: Learn the Word™

Unwrap the mysteries of Revelation in this Biblically-Inept™ brand of simplified Bible commentaries for teens. Don't sweat the future. Learn everything God wants you to know about what's going to happen, including the Rapture, the Tribulation, the Antichrist, and the new heaven and earth. New features, including "Happenings" and "Stop," are combined with popular elements from the adult series, such as "Key Symbols," definitions, illustrations, and study questions.

(trade paper)   ISBN 1892016559   **$14.99**

Don't Miss These Popular Web Sites!

www.biblicallyinept.com
www.sundayschoolteach.com
www.homeschoolteach.com
www.learntheword.com

Purchasing Information

www.starburstpublishers.com

Books are available from your favorite bookstore, either from current stock or special order. To assist bookstores in locating your selection, be sure to give title, author, and ISBN. If unable to purchase from a bookstore, you may order direct from STARBURST PUBLISHERS. When ordering please enclose full payment plus shipping and handling as follows:

Post Office (4th class)
$4.00 with a purchase of up to $20.00
$5.00 ($20.01–$50.00)
9% of purchase price for purchases of $50.01 and up

Canada
$5.00 (up to $35.00)
15% ($35.01 and up)

United Parcel Service (UPS)
$5.00 (up to $20.00)
$7.00 ($20.01–$50.00)
12% ($50.01 and up)

Overseas
$5.00 (up to $25.00)
20% ($25.01 and up)

Payment in U.S. funds only. Please allow two to four weeks minimum for delivery by USPS (longer for overseas and Canada). Allow two to seven working days for delivery by UPS. Make checks payable to and mail to:

Starburst Publishers®
P.O. Box 4123
Lancaster, PA 17604

Credit card orders may be placed by calling 1-800-441-1456, Mon.–Fri., 8:30 A.M. to 5:30 P.M. Eastern Standard Time. Prices are subject to change without notice. For a catalog send a 9 x 12 self-addressed envelope with four first-class stamps.